CAPE PLAYS

THE VISIT

FRIEDRICH DÜRRENMATT

THE VISIT
a tragi-comedy

Translated from the German by
PATRICK BOWLES

JONATHAN CAPE
LONDON

Translated from the German *Der Besuch der Alten Dame*
© 1956 by Peter Schifferli, Verlags AG 'Die Arche', Zurich
This translation first published in Great Britain 1962
Reissued in this format 1973

25 27 29 30 28 26 24

This translation © 1962 by Jonathan Cape Ltd

Jonathan Cape, 20 Vauxhall Bridge Road, London SW1V 2SA

ISBN 9780224009140

Printed and bound in Great Britain by
Cox & Wyman Ltd, Reading, Berkshire

TRANSLATOR'S FOREWORD

A translator's task is to render another person's ideas into acceptable language, and his aim is to find some equivalent to the original unity of thought and speech. This simple definition may lead to unexpected results. Some years ago it was my privilege to work with Samuel Beckett on the English version of his French novel, *Molloy*. From the outset he stressed that it shouldn't merely be 'translated': we should write a new book in the new language. For with the transposition of speech occurs a transposition of thought and even, at times, of action: 'You wouldn't *say* exactly that, in English, you'd say something else.' It shouldn't be merely a matter of setting up new signposts. To interpret a foreign book one must hope for some intuition as to how its material might have occurred in one's own mental landscape, wherewith to re-create in the new language. One translates within the dilemma of literalness and readability, the one tending to rise as the other falls, and vice versa. The play which follows is a translation, not an adaptation. The import and intention of the German were my first preoccupation, but I should make two qualifying remarks: I have been impelled by the different verse-traditions in Germany and England to transpose the irregular, occasionally alliterative 'free verse' of the final chorus into more measured lines. So rendered, with timed caesurae, etc., they seem (I hope) to have more punch, and be more suited to the English stage with its special background of dramatic poetry, than if rendered into loose 'free' verse of the kind associated with the 'twenties and 'thirties. And various other speeches have been set in idioms which do not exist in Germany yet seemed a feasible Anglo–American dramatist's choice I have tried to avoid taking licence with their sense.

The Visit is a macabre parable and may deserve an essay, but it makes sufficiently easy reading for both common and uncommon readers not to need one; I have only wished to note technical points relevant to their conception of the original.

The title of the first English stage production of *The Visit* (with which this translator has remained unfamiliar) has been retained, at the publisher's request. The text followed was the complete one: *Der Besuch der Alten Dame* — literally, *The Visit of the Old Lady* — published by Verlag AG. 'Die Arche,' Zürich, 1956.

PATRICK BOWLES

THE VISIT

CHARACTERS

Visitors:

    Claire Zachanassian, née Wascher, multi-millionairess, Armenian Oil

    Her Husbands, VII–IX

    Butler

    Toby ⎫
    Roby ⎬ gum-chewers
    Koby ⎫
    Loby ⎬ blind

Visited:

    Ill

    His wife

    His son

    His daughter

    Mayor

    Priest

    Schoolmaster

    Doctor

    Policeman

    Man One

    Man Two

    Man Three

    Man Four

    Painter

    First woman

    Second woman

    Miss Louisa

Extras:
    Station-master
    Ticket Inspector
    Guard
    Bailiff

Distractors:
    First Reporter
    Second Reporter
    Radio Commentator
    Cameraman

PLACE: Guellen, a Smalltown

TIME: the Present

(Interval after Act Two)

ACT ONE

Clangor of railway-station bell before curtain rises to discover legend: 'Guellen'. Obviously name of small, skimpily depicted township in background: a tumbledown wreck. Equally ramshackle station-buildings may or may not be cordoned off, according to country, and include a rusty signal-cabin, its door marked 'No Entry'. Also depicted in bare outline, centre, the piteous Station Road. Left, a barren little building with tiled roof and mutilated posters on its windowless walls. A sign, at left corner: 'Ladies'. Another, at right corner: 'Gents'. This entire prospect steeped in hot autumn sun. In front of little building, a bench. On it, four men. An unspeakably ragged fifth (so are the other four) is inscribing letters in red paint on a banner clearly intended for some procession: 'Welcome Clarie'. Thunderous pounding din of express train rushing through. Men on bench show interest in express train by following its headlong rush with head movements from left to right.

MAN ONE. The Gudrun. Hamburg–Naples.

MAN TWO. The Racing Roland gets here at eleven twenty-seven. Venice–Stockholm.

MAN THREE. Our last remaining pleasure: watching trains go by.

MAN FOUR. Five years ago the Gudrun and the Racing Roland stopped in Guellen. And the Diplomat. And the Lorelei. All famous express trains.

MAN ONE. World famous.

MAN TWO. Now not even the commuting trains stop. Just two from Kaffigen and the one-thirteen from Kalberstadt.

MAN THREE. Ruined.

MAN FOUR. The Wagner Factory gone crash.

~~MAN ONE. Bockmann bankrupt.~~

MAN TWO. The Foundry on Sunshine Square shut down.

MAN THREE. Living on the dole.

MAN FOUR. On Poor Relief soup.

MAN ONE. Living?

MAN TWO. Vegetating.

MAN THREE. And rotting to death.

MAN FOUR. The entire township.

(*Bell rings.*)

MAN TWO. It's more than time that millionairess got here. They say she founded a hospital in Kalberstadt.

MAN THREE. And a kindergarten in Kaffigen. ~~And a memorial chusch in the Capital.~~

PAINTER. She had Zimt do her portrait. That Naturalistic dauber.

MAN ONE. She and her money. She owns Armenian Oil, Western Railways, North Broadcasting Company and the Hong Kong — uh — Amusement District.

(*Train clatter. Station-master salutes. Men move heads from right to left after train.*)

MAN FOUR. The Diplomat.

MAN THREE. We were a city of the Arts, then.

MAN TWO. One of the foremost in the land.

MAN ONE. In Europe.

MAN FOUR. Goethe spent a night here. In the Golden Apostle.

MAN THREE. Brahms composed a quartet here.

(*Bell rings.*)

MAN TWO. Bertold Schwarz invented gunpowder here.

PAINTER. And I was a brilliant student at the Ecole des Beaux Arts. And what am I doing here now? Sign-painting!

(*Train clatter. Guard appears, left, as after jumping off train.*)

GUARD (*long-drawn wail*). Guëllen!

MAN ONE. The Kaffigen commuter.

(*One passenger has got off, left. He walks past men on bench, disappears through doorway marked 'Gents'.*)

MAN TWO. The Bailiff.

MAN THREE. Going to distrain on the Town Hall.

MAN FOUR. We're even ruined politically.

STATION-MASTER (waves green flag, blows whistle). Stand clear!

    (Enter from town, Mayor, Schoolmaster, Priest and Ill —
    a man of near sixty-five; all shabbily dressed.)

MAYOR. The guest of honour will be arriving on the one-
    thirteen commuter from Kalberstadt.

SCHOOLMASTER. We'll have the mixed choir singing; the
    Youth Club.

PRIEST. And the fire bell ringing. It hasn't been pawned.

MAYOR. We'll have the town band playing on Market Square.
    The Athletics Club will honour the millionairess with a
    pyramid. Then a meal in the Golden Apostle. Finances
    unfortunately can't be stretched to illuminating the
    Cathedral for the evening. Or the Town Hall.

    (Bailiff comes out of little building.)

BAILIFF. Good morning, Mister Mayor, a very good morning
    to you.

MAYOR. Why, Mister Glutz, what are you doing here?

BAILIFF. You know my mission, Mister Mayor. It's a colossal
    undertaking I'm faced with. Just you try distraining on an
    entire town.

MAYOR. You won't find a thing in the Town Hall. Apart from
    one old typewriter.

BAILIFF. I think you're forgetting something, Mister Mayor.
    The Guellen History Museum.

MAYOR. Gone three years ago. Sold to America. Our coffers
    are empty. Not a single soul pays taxes.

BAILIFF. It'll have to be investigated. The country's booming,
    and Guellen has the Sunshine Foundry. But Guellen goes
    bankrupt.

MAYOR. We're up against a real economic enigma.

MAN ONE. The whole thing's a Free Masons' plot.

MAN TWO. Conspired by the Jews.

MAN THREE. Backed by High Finance.

MAN FOUR. ~~International Communism's showing its colours.~~

(*Bell rings.*)

BAILIFF. I always find something. I've got eyes like a hawk. I think I'll take a look at the Treasury.

(*Exit.*)

MAYOR. Better let him plunder us first. Not after the mil- ~~lionairess's visit.~~

(*Painter has finished painting his banner.*)

ILL. You know, Mister Mayor, that won't do. This banner's too familiar. It ought to read, 'Welcome Claire Zachanassian'.

MAN ONE. But she's Clarie!

MAN TWO. Clarie Wascher!

MAN THREE. She was educated here!

MAN FOUR. Her dad was the builder.

PAINTER. O.K., so I'll write 'Welcome Claire Zachanassian' on the back. Then if the millionairess seems touched we can turn it round and show her the front.

MAN TWO. It's the Speculator. Zürich-Hamburg.

(*Another express train passes. Right to left.*)

MAN THREE. Always on time, you can set your watch by it.

MAN FOUR. ~~Tell me who still owns a watch in this place.~~

MAYOR. Gentlemen, the millionairess is our only hope.

PRIEST. Apart from God.

MAYOR. Apart from God.

SCHOOLMASTER. But God won't pay.

MAYOR. You used to be a friend of hers, Ill, so now it all depends on you.

PRIEST. But their ways parted. I heard some story about it — have you no confession to make to your Priest?

ILL. We were the best of friends. Young and hotheaded. I used to be a bit of a lad, gentlemen, forty-five years ago. And she, Clara, I can see her still: coming towards me through the shadows in Petersens' Barn, all aglow. Or walking barefoot in the Konrad's Village Wood, over the moss and the leaves, with her red hair streaming out, slim and supple as a willow, and tender, ah, what a devilish beautiful little witch. Life tore us apart. Life. That's the way it is.

MAYOR. I ought to have a few details about Madam Zachanassian for my little after-dinner speech in the Golden Apostle. (*Takes a small notebook from pocket.*)

SCHOOLMASTER. I've been going through the old school-reports. Clara Wascher's marks, I'm sorry to say, were appalling. So was her conduct. She only passed in botany and zoology.

MAYOR (*takes note*). Good. Botany and zoology. A pass. That's good.

ILL. I can help you here, Mister Mayor. Clara loved justice. Most decidedly. Once when they took a beggar away she flung stones at the police.

MAYOR. Love of justice. Not bad. It always works. But I think we'd better leave out that bit about the police.

ILL. She was generous too. Everything she had she shared. She stole potatoes once for an old widow woman.

MAYOR. ~~Sense of generosity. Gentlemen, I absolutely must bring that in.~~ It's the crucial point. ~~Does anyone here remember a building her father built? That'd sound good in my speech.~~

ALL. ~~No. No. No. No one.~~

(*Mayor shuts his little notebook.*)

MAYOR. I'm fully prepared, for my part. The rest is up to Ill.

ILL. I know. Zachanassian has to cough up her millions.

MAYOR. Millions — that's the idea. Precisely.

SCHOOLMASTER. It won't help us if she only founds a nursery.

MAYOR. My dear Ill, you've been the most popular personality in Guellen for a long while now. In the spring, I shall be retiring. I've sounded out the Opposition: we've agreed to nominate you as my successor.

ILL. But Mister Mayor.

SCHOOLMASTER. I can confirm that.

ILL. Gentlemen, back to business. First of all, I'll tell Clara all about our wretched plight.

PRIEST. But do be careful — do be tactful.

ILL. We've got to be clever. Psychologically acute. If we make a fiasco of the welcome at the station, we could easily wreck everything else. ~~You won't bring it off by relying on the municipal band and the mixed choir.~~

MAYOR. Ill's right, there. It'll be one of the decisive moments. Madam Zachanassian sets foot on her native soil, she's home again, and how moved she is, there are tears in her eyes, ah, the old familiar places. The old faces. Not that I'll be standing here like this in my shirt-sleeves. I'll be wearing my formal black and a top hat. My wife beside me, my two grandchildren in front of me, all in white. Holding roses. My God, if only it all works out according to plan!

(Bell rings.)

MAN ONE. It's the Racing Roland.

MAN TWO. Venice-Stockholm eleven twenty-seven.

PRIEST. Eleven twenty-seven! We still have nearly two hours to get suitably dressed.

MAYOR. Kuhn and Hauser hoist the 'Welcome Claire Zachanassian' banner. (Points at four men.) You others better wave your hats. ~~But please: no bawling like last year at the Government Mission, it hardly impressed them~~ at all and so far we've had no subsidy. This is no time for wild enthusiasm, the mood you want is an inward, an almost tearful sympathy for one of our children, who was lost, and has been found again. Be relaxed. Sincere. But above all, time it well. The instant the choir stops singing, sound the fire-alarm. And look out . . .

(*His speech is drowned by thunder of oncoming train.
Squealing brakes. Dumbfounded astonishment on all faces.
The five men spring up from bench.*)

PAINTER. Thé Express!

MAN ONE. It's stopping!

MAN TWO. In Guellen!

MAN THREE. The lousiest —

MAN FOUR. Most poverty-stricken —

MAN ONE. Desolate dump on the Venice-Stockholm line!

STATION-MASTER. It's against the Laws of Nature. ~~The Racing
Roland ought to materialize from around the Leutheneu
Pond~~, roar through Guellen, dwindle into a dark dot over
at Plückenried valley and vanish.

(*Enter, right, Claire Zachanassian. Sixty-three, red hair,
pearl necklace, enormous gold bangles, unbelievably got up
to kill and yet by the same token a Society Lady with a rare
grace, in spite of all the grotesquerie. Followed by her
entourage, comprising Butler Boby, aged about eighty,
wearing dark glasses, and Husband VII, tall and thin with a
black moustache, sporting a complete angler's outfit. Accompanying this group, an excited Ticket Inspector, peaked cap,
little red satchel.*)

CLAIRE ZACHANASSIAN. Is it Guellen?

TICKET INSPECTOR. Madam. You pulled the Emergency Brake.

CLAIRE ZACHANASSIAN. I always pull the Emergency Brake.

TICKET INSPECTOR. I protest. Vigorously. No one ever pulls the
Emergency Brake in this country. Not even in case of
emergency. Our first duty is to our time-table. ~~Will you
kindly give me an explanation.~~

CLAIRE ZACHANASSIAN. It is Guellen, Moby. I recognize the
wretched dump. That's Konrad's Village Wood, yonder,
with a stream you can fish — pike and trout; that roof on
the right is Petersens' Barn.

ILL (*as if awakening*). Clara.

SCHOOLMASTER. Madam Zachanassian.

ALL. Madam Zachanassian.

SCHOOLMASTER. And the choir and the Youth Club aren't ready!

MAYOR. The Athletics Club! The Fire Brigade!

PRIEST. The Sexton!

MAYOR. My frock-coat, for God's sake, my top hat, my grandchildren!

MAN ONE. Clarie Wascher's here! Clarie Wascher's here!
    (*Jumps up, rushes off towards town.*)

MAYOR (*calling after him*). Don't forget my wife!

TICKET INSPECTOR. I'm waiting for an explanation. In my official capacity. I represent the Railway Management.

CLAIRE ZACHANASSIAN. ~~You're a simpleton.~~ I want to pay this little town a visit. ~~What d'you expect me to do, hop off your express train?~~

TICKET INSPECTOR. You stopped the Racing Roland just because you wanted to visit Guellen?

CLAIRE ZACHANASSIAN. Of course.

TICKET INSPECTOR. Madam. Should you desire to visit Guellen, the twelve-forty commuter from Kalberstadt is at your service. Please use it. Like other people. ~~Arrival in Guellen one thirteen p.m.~~

CLAIRE ZACHANASSIAN. The ordinary passenger train? ~~The one that stops in Loken, Brunnhübel, Beisenbach and Leuthenau? Are you really and truly asking me to go puffing round this countryside for half an hour?~~

TICKET INSPECTOR. You'll pay for this, Madam. Dearly.

CLAIRE ZACHANASSIAN. Boby, give him a thousand.

ALL (*murmuring*). A thousand.
    (*Butler gives Ticket Inspector a thousand.*)

TICKET INSPECTOR (*perplexed*). Madam.

CLAIRE ZACHANASSIAN. And three thousand for the Railway Widows' Fund.

18

ALL (*murmuring*). Three thousand.
> (*Ticket Inspector receives three thousand from Butler.*)

TICKET INSPECTOR (*staggered*). Madam. No such fund exists.

CLAIRE ZACHANASSIAN. Then found one.
> (*The supreme Civic Authority whispers a word or two in Ticket Inspector's ear.*)

TICKET INSPECTOR (*all confusion*). Madam is Madam Claire Zachanassian? O do excuse me. Of course it's different in that case. We'd have been only too happy to stop in Guellen if we'd had the faintest notion, O, here's your money back, Madam, four thousand, my God.

ALL (*murmuring*). Four thousand.

CLAIRE ZACHANASSIAN. Keep it, it's nothing.

ALL (*murmuring*). Keep it.

TICKET INSPECTOR. Does Madam require the Racing Roland to wait while she visits Guellen? I know the Railway Management would be only too glad. They say the Cathedral portals are well worth a look. Gothic. With the Last Judgment.

CLAIRE ZACHANASSIAN. Will you and your express train get the hell out of here?

HUSBAND VII (*whines*). But the Press, poppet, the Press haven't got off yet. The Reporters have no idea. They're dining up front in the saloon.

CLAIRE ZACHANASSIAN. Let them dine, Moby, let them dine. I can't use the Press in Guellen yet, and they'll come back later on, don't worry.
> (*Meanwhile Man Two has brought Mayor his frock-coat. Mayor crosses ceremoniously to Claire Zachanassian. Painter and Man Four stand on bench, hoist banner: 'Welcome Claire Zachanassi' ... Painter did not quite finish it.*)

STATION-MASTER (*whistles, waves green flag*). Stand clear!

TICKET INSPECTOR. I do trust you won't complain to the

Railway Management, Madam. It was a pure misunderstanding.

(*Train begins moving out. Ticket Inspector jumps on.*)

MAYOR. Madam Zachanassian, my dear lady. As Mayor of Guellen, it is my honour to welcome you, a child of our native town ...

(*Remainder of Mayor's speech drowned in clatter of express train as it begins to move and then to race away. He speaks doggedly on.*)

CLAIRE ZACHANASSIAN. I must thank you, Mister Mayor, for your fine speech.

(*She crosses to Ill who, somewhat embarrassed, has moved towards her.*)

ILL. Clara.

CLAIRE ZACHANASSIAN. Alfred.

ILL. It's nice you've come.

CLAIRE ZACHANASSIAN. I'd always planned to. All my life. Ever since I left Guellen.

ILL (*unsure of himself*). It's sweet of you.

CLAIRE ZACHANASSIAN. Did you think about me too?

ILL. Of course. All the time. You know I did, Clara.

CLAIRE ZACHANASSIAN. They were wonderful, all those days we used to spend together.

ILL (*proudly*). They sure were. (*to Schoolmaster*) See, Professor, I've got her in the bag.

CLAIRE ZACHANASSIAN. Call me what you always used to call me.

ILL. My little wildcat.

CLAIRE ZACHANASSIAN (*purrs like an old cat*). And what else?

ILL. My little sorceress.

CLAIRE ZACHANASSIAN. I used to call you my black panther.

ILL. I still am.

CLAIRE ZACHANASSIAN. Rubbish. You've grown fat. And grey. And drink-sodden.

ILL. But *you're* still the same, my little sorceress.

CLAIRE ZACHANASSIAN. Don't be daft. I've grown old and fat as well. And lost my left leg. An automobile accident. Now I only travel in express trains. But they made a splendid job of the artificial one, don't you think? (*She pulls up her skirt, displays left leg.*) It bends very well.

ILL (*wipes away sweat*). But my little wildcat, I'd never have noticed it.

CLAIRE ZACHANASSIAN. Would you like to meet my seventh husband, Alfred? Tobacco Plantations. We're very happily married.

ILL. But by all means.

CLAIRE ZACHANASSIAN. Come on, Moby, come and make your bow. As a matter of fact his name's Pedro, but Moby's much nicer. In any case it goes better with Boby; that's the butler's name. And you get your butlers for life, so husbands have to be christened accordingly.

(*Husband* VII *bows.*)

Isn't he nice, with his little black moustache? Think it over, Moby.

(*Husband* VII *thinks it over.*)

Harder.

(*Husband* VII *thinks it over harder.*)

Harder still.

HUSBAND VII. But I can't think any harder, poppet, really I can't.

CLAIRE ZACHANASSIAN. Of course you can. Just try.

(*Husband* VII *thinks harder still. Bell rings.*)

You see. It works. Don't you agree, Alfred, he looks almost demoniacal like that. Like a Brazilian. But no! He's Greek-Orthodox. His father was Russian. We were married by a Pope. Most interesting. Now I'm going to have a look round Guellen.

21

(She inspects little house, left, through jewel-encrusted lorgnette.)

My father built this Public Convenience, Moby. Good work, painstakingly executed. When I was a child I spent hours on that roof, spitting. But only on the Gents.

(Mixed choir and Youth Club have now assembled in background. Schoolmaster steps forward wearing top hat.)

SCHOOLMASTER. Madam. As Headmaster of Guellen College, and lover of the noblest Muse, may I take the liberty of offering you a homely folk-song, rendered by the mixed choir and the Youth Club.

CLAIRE ZACHANASSIAN. Fire away, Schoolmaster, let's hear your homely folk-song.

(Schoolmaster takes up tuning-fork, strikes key. Mixed choir and Youth Club begin ceremoniously singing, at which juncture another train arrives, left. Station-master salutes. Choir struggles against cacophonous clatter of train, Schoolmaster despairs, train, at long last, passes.)

MAYOR *(despondent)*. The fire alarm, sound the fire alarm!

CLAIRE ZACHANASSIAN. Well sung, Guelleners! That blond bass out there on the left, with the big Adam's apple, he was really most singular.

(A Policeman elbows a passage through mixed choir, draws up to attention in front of Claire Zachanassian.)

POLICEMAN. Police Inspector Hahncke, Madam. At your service.

CLAIRE ZACHANASSIAN *(inspects him)*. Thank you. I shan't want to arrest anybody. But Guellen may need you soon. Can you wink a blind eye to things from time to time?

POLICEMAN. Sure I can, Madam. Where would I be in Guellen if I couldn't!

CLAIRE ZACHANASSIAN. Start learning to wink them both.

(Policeman goggles at her, perplexed.)

ILL *(laughing)*. Just like Clara! Just like my little wildcat!

(*Slaps thigh with enjoyment. Mayor perches Schoolmaster's top hat on his own head, ushers pair of grandchildren forward. Twin seven-year-old girls, blond plaits.*)

MAYOR. My grandchildren, Madam. Hermione and Adolfina. My wife is the only one not present.

(*Mops perspiration. The two little girls curtsy for Madam Zachanassian and offer her red roses.*)

CLAIRE ZACHANASSIAN. Congratulations on your kids, Mister Mayor. Here!

(*She bundles roses into Station-master's arms. Mayor stealthily hands top hat to Priest, who puts it on.*)

MAYOR. Our Priest, Madam.

(*Priest raises top hat, bows.*)

CLAIRE ZACHANASSIAN. Ah, the Priest. Do you comfort the dying?

PRIEST (*startled*). I do what I can.

CLAIRE ZACHANASSIAN. People who've been condemned to death as well?

PRIEST (*perplexed*). The death sentence has been abolished in this country, Madam.

CLAIRE ZACHANASSIAN. It may be reintroduced.

(*Priest, with some consternation, returns top hat to Mayor, who dons it again.*)

ILL (*laughing*). Really, little wildcat! You crack the wildest jokes.

CLAIRE ZACHANASSIAN. Now I want to go into town.

(*Mayor attempts to offer her his arm.*)

What's all this, Mister Mayor. I don't go hiking miles on my artificial leg.

MAYOR (*shocked*). Immediately, immediately, Madam. The doctor owns a car. It's a Mercedes. The nineteen thirty-two model.

POLICEMAN (*clicking heels*). I'll see to it, Mister Mayor. I'll have the car commandeered and driven round.

CLAIRE ZACHANASSIAN. That won't be necessary. Since my accident I only go about in sedan-chairs. Roby, Toby, bring it here.

(*Enter, left, two herculean gum-chewing brutes with sedan-chair. One of them has a guitar slung at his back.*)

Two gangsters. From Manhattan. They were on their way to ~~Sing-Sing~~. To the electric chair. I petitioned for them to be freed as sedan-bearers. Cost me a million dollars per petition. The sedan-chair came from the Louvre. A gift from the French President. Such a nice man; ~~he looks exactly like his pictures in the newspapers~~. Roby, Toby, take me into town.

ROBY/TOBY (*in unison*). Yes Mam.

CLAIRE ZACHANASSIAN. But first of all to the Petersens' Barn, and then to Konrad's Village Wood. I want to take Alfred to visit our old trysting-places. In the meanwhile have the luggage and the coffin put in the Golden Apostle.

MAYOR (*startled*). The coffin?

CLAIRE ZACHANASSIAN. Yes, I brought a coffin with me. I may need it. Roby, Toby, off we go!

(*The pair of gum-chewing brutes carry Claire Zachanassian away to town. Mayor gives signal, whereon all burst into cheers which spontaneously fade as two more servants enter, bearing an elaborate black coffin, cross stage and exeunt, towards Guellen. Now, undaunted and unpawned, the fire-alarm bell starts ringing.*)

MAYOR. At last! The fire bell.

(*Populace gather round coffin. It is followed in by Claire Zachanassian's maidservants and an endless stream of cases and trunks, carried by Guelleners. This traffic is controlled by Police-man, who is about to follow it out when enter at that point a pair of little old fat soft-spoken men, both impeccably dressed.*)

THE PAIR. We're in Guellen. We can smell it, we can smell it, we can smell it in the air, in the Guellen air.

24

POLICEMAN. And who might you be?

THE PAIR. We belong to the old lady, we belong to the old lady. She calls us Koby and Loby.

POLICEMAN. Madam Zachanassian is staying at the Golden Apostle.

THE PAIR (*gay*). We're blind, we're blind.

POLICEMAN. Blind? O.K., I'll take you there, in duplicate.

THE PAIR. O thank you Mister Policeman, thank you very much.

POLICEMAN (*with surprise*). If you're blind, how did you know I was a policeman?

THE PAIR. By your tone of voice, your tone of voice, all policemen have the same tone of voice.

POLICEMAN (*with suspicion*). You fat little men seem to have had a bit of contact with the police.

THE PAIR (*incredulous*). Men, he thinks we're men!

POLICEMAN. Then what the hell are you?

THE PAIR. You'll soon see, you'll soon see!

POLICEMAN (*baffled*). Well, you seem cheerful about it.

THE PAIR. We get steak and ham, every day, every day.

POLICEMAN. Yeah. I'd get up and dance for that too. Come on, give me your hands. Funny kind of humour foreigners have. (*Goes off to town with pair.*)

THE PAIR. Off to Boby and Moby, off to Roby and Toby!

(*Open scene-change: façade of station and adjacent little building soar into flies. Interior of the Golden Apostle: an hotel-sign might well be let down from above, an imposing gilded Apostle, as emblem, and left to hang in mid-air. Faded, outmoded luxury. Everything threadbare, tattered, dusty and musty and gone to seed. Interminable processions of porters taking interminable pieces of luggage upstairs: first a cage, then the cases and trunks. Mayor and Schoolmaster seated in foreground drinking Schnapps.*)

MAYOR. Cases, cases, and still more cases. Mountains of them. And a little while ago they came in with a cage. There was a panther in it. A black, wild animal.

SCHOOLMASTER. She had the coffin put in a special spare room. Curious.

MAYOR. Famous women have their whims and fancies.

SCHOOLMASTER. She seems to want to stay here quite a while.

MAYOR. So much the better. Ill has her in the bag. He was calling her his little wildcat, his little sorceress. He'll get thousands out of her. Her health, Professor. ~~And may Claire Zachanassian restore the Bockmann business.~~

SCHOOLMASTER. ~~And the Wagner Factory.~~

MAYOR. ~~And the Foundry on Sunshine Square. If they boom we'll all boom — my Community and your College and the Standard of Living.~~

(*He has called a toast; they clink glasses.*)

SCHOOLMASTER. I've been correcting the Guellen school-children's Latin and Greek exercises for more than two decades, Mister Mayor, but let me tell you, Sir, I only learned what horror is one hour ago. That old lady in black robes getting off the train was a gruesome vision. Like one of the Fates; she made me think of an avenging Greek goddess. ~~Her name shouldn't be Claire; it should be Clotho. I could suspect her of spinning destiny's webs herself.~~

(*Enter Policeman. Hangs cap on peg.*)

MAYOR. Pull up a chair, Inspector.

(*Policeman pulls up a chair.*)

— POLICEMAN. Not much fun patrolling in this dump. But maybe now it'll rise from the ashes. I've just been to Petersens' Barn with the millionairess and that shopkeeper Ill. I witnessed a moving scene. Both parties maintained a meditative pause, as in church. I was embarrassed. I therefore did not follow them when they went to Konrad's

Village Wood. Say, that was a real procession. The sedan-chair first, then Ill walking beside it, then the Butler, then her seventh husband last with his fishing-rod.

SCHOOLMASTER. That conspicuous consumption of husbands; ~~she's a second Lais.~~

POLICEMAN. And those two little fat men. ~~The devil knows what it all means.~~

SCHOOLMASTER. Sinister. ~~An ascent from the infernal regions.~~

MAYOR. I wonder what they're after, in Konrad's Village Wood.

POLICEMAN. The same as in Petersens' Barn, Mister Mayor. They're calling in on the places where their passion used to burn, as they say.

~~SCHOOLMASTER. Flame, flame. Remember Shakespeare: Romeo and Juliet. Gentlemen: I'm stirred. I sense the grandeur of antiquity in Guellen. I've never sensed it here before.~~

MAYOR. Gentlemen: we must drink a special toast to Ill — a man who's doing all a man can to better our lot. To our most popular citizen: to my successor!

(*The Hotel Apostle floats away, back into the flies. Enter the four citizens, left, with a simple, backless wooden bench, which they set down, left. Man One, with a huge, paste-board heart hanging from his neck, on it the letters A $\updownarrow$ C, climbs on to the bench. The others stand round him in a half-circle, holding twigs at arm's length to designate trees.*)

MAN ONE.
We are trees, we're pine and spruce
MAN TWO.
We are beech, and dark-green fir
MAN THREE.
Lichen, moss and climbing ivy
MAN FOUR.
Undergrowth and lair of fox

MAN ONE.

Drifting cloud and call of bird

MAN TWO.

We are the woodland wilderness

MAN THREE.

Toadstool, and the timid deer

MAN FOUR.

And rustling leaves; and bygone dreams.

(*The two gum-chewing brutes emerge from background bearing sedan-chair with Claire Zachanassian, Ill at her side. Behind her, Husband VII. Butler brings up rear, leading blind pair by the hand.*)

CLAIRE ZACHANASSIAN. It's the Konrad's Village Wood. Roby, Toby, stop a moment.

BLIND PAIR. Stop, Roby and Toby, stop, Boby and Moby.

(*Claire Zachanassian descends from sedan-chair, surveys wood.*)

CLAIRE ZACHANASSIAN. There's the heart with our two names on it, Alfred. Almost faded away, and grown apart. And the tree's grown. The trunk and branches have thickened. The way we have ourselves.

(*Claire Zachanassian crosses to other trees.*)

A woodland bower. It's a long time since I last walked through these woods, in my young days, frolicking in the foliage and the purple ivy. You brutes just go and chew your gum behind the bushes, and take your sedan-chair with you; I don't want to look at your mugs all the time. And Moby, stroll away over to that stream on the right, there, and look at the fish.

(*Exit brutes, left, with sedan-chair. Exit Husband VII, right. Claire Zachanassian sits on bench.*)

Look, a doe.

(*Man Three springs off.*)

28

ILL. ~~It's the close season.~~

(*Sits next to her.*)

CLAIRE ZACHANASSIAN. We kissed each other on this spot. More than fifty years ago. We loved each other under these boughs, under these bushes, among these toadstools on the moss. I was seventeen, and you weren't quite twenty. Then you married Matilda Blumhard with her little general store, and I married old Zachanassian with his millions from Armenia. He found me in a brothel. In Hamburg. It was my red hair took his fancy; the old, gold lecher!

ILL. Clara!

CLAIRE ZACHANASSIAN. Boby, a Henry Clay.

BLIND PAIR. A Henry Clay, a Henry Clay.

(*Butler comes out of background, passes her a cigar, lights it.*)

CLAIRE ZACHANASSIAN. I'm fond of cigars. I suppose I ought to smoke my husband's produce; but I don't trust them.

ILL. It was for your sake I married Matilda Blumhard.

CLAIRE ZACHANASSIAN. She had money.

ILL. You were young and beautiful. The future belonged to you. I wanted you to be happy. So I had to renounce being happy myself.

CLAIRE ZACHANASSIAN. And now the future's here.

ILL. If you'd stayed here, you'd have been ruined like me.

CLAIRE ZACHANASSIAN. Are you ruined?

ILL. A broken-down shopkeeper in a broken-down town.

CLAIRE ZACHANASSIAN. Now it's me who has money.

ILL. I've been living in hell since you went away from me.

CLAIRE ZACHANASSIAN. And I've grown into hell itself.

ILL. Always rowing with my family. They blame me for being poor.

CLAIRE ZACHANASSIAN. Didn't little Matilda make you happy?

ILL. Your happiness is what matters.

CLAIRE ZACHANASSIAN. Your children?

ILL. No sense of ideals.

CLAIRE ZACHANASSIAN. They'll develop one soon.

(*He says nothing. Both gaze at the wood of childhood memory.*)

ILL. I lead a laughable life. Never once really managed to leave this township. One trip to Berlin and one to Tessin. That's all.

CLAIRE ZACHANASSIAN. Why bother, anyway. I know what the world's like.

ILL. Because you've always been able to travel.

CLAIRE ZACHANASSIAN. Because I own it.

(*He says nothing; she smokes.*)

ILL. Everything's going to be different now.

CLAIRE ZACHANASSIAN. Sure.

ILL (*watches her*). Are you going to help us?

CLAIRE ZACHANASSIAN. I shan't leave my home-town in the lurch.

ILL. We need thousands.

CLAIRE ZACHANASSIAN. That's nothing.

ILL (*enthusiastically*). My little wildcat!

(*Moved, he slaps her on left shoulder, then painfully withdraws hand.*)

CLAIRE ZACHANASSIAN. That hurt. You hit one of the straps for my artificial leg.

(*Man One pulls pipe and rusty door-key from trousers-pocket, taps on pipe with key.*)

A woodpecker.

ILL. Now it's the way it used to be when we were young and bold, when we went out walking in Konrad's Village Wood, in the days of our young love. And the sun was a dazzling orb, above the pine-trees. And far away a few wisps of cloud, and somewhere in the woodland you could hear a cuckoo calling.

MAN FOUR. Cuckoo, cuckoo!

(Ill lays hand on Man One.)

ILL. Cool wood, and the wind in the boughs, soughing like the sea-surge.

(The three men who are trees begin soughing and blowing and waving their arms up and down.)

Ah, my little sorceress, if only time had really dissolved. If only life hadn't put us asunder.

CLAIRE ZACHANASSIAN. Would you wish that?

ILL. That above all, above all. I do love you!

(Kisses her right hand.)

The same, cool white hand.

CLAIRE ZACHANASSIAN. No, you're wrong. It's artificial too. Ivory.

(Ill, horrified, releases her hand.)

ILL. Clara, are you all artificial?

CLAIRE ZACHANASSIAN. Practically. My plane crashed in Afghanistan. I was the only one who crawled out of the wreckage. Even the crew died. I'm unkillable.

BLIND PAIR. She's unkillable, she's unkillable.

(Ceremonial oom-pah music. The Hotel Apostle descends again. Guelleners bring in tables, wretched, tattered table-cloths, cutlery, crockery, food. One table, centre, one left, and one right, parallel to audience. Priest comes out of back-ground. More Guelleners flock in, among them a Gymnast. Mayor, Schoolmaster and Policeman reappear.
The Guelleners applaud. Mayor crosses to bench where Claire Zachanassian and Ill are sitting; the trees have metamor-phosed back into citizens and moved away upstage.)

MAYOR. The storm of applause is for you, my dear lady.

CLAIRE ZACHANASSIAN. It's for the town band, Mister Mayor. It was a capital performance; and the Athletics Club did a wonderful pyramid. I love men in shorts and vests. They look so natural.

MAYOR. May I escort you to your place?
(He escorts Claire Zachanassian to her place at table, centre, introduces her to his wife.)
My wife.
(Claire Zachanassian examines wife through lorgnette.)

CLAIRE ZACHANASSIAN. Annie Dummermut, top of our class.
(Mayor introduces her to a second woman, as worn out and embittered as his wife.)

MAYOR. Mrs Ill.

CLAIRE ZACHANASSIAN. Matilda Blumhard. I can remember you lying in wait for Alfred behind the shop door. You've grown very thin and pale, my dear.
(Doctor hurries in, right; a squat, thick-set fifty-year-old; moustachioed, bristly black hair, scarred face, threadbare frock-coat.)

DOCTOR. Just managed to do it, in my old Mercedes.

MAYOR. Doctor Nuesslin, our physician.
(Claire Zachanassian examines Doctor through lorgnette as he kisses her hand.)

CLAIRE ZACHANASSIAN. Interesting. Do you make out Death Certificates?

DOCTOR *(taken off guard)*. Death Certificates?

CLAIRE ZACHANASSIAN. If someone should die?

DOCTOR. Of course, Madam. It's my duty. As decreed by the authorities.

CLAIRE ZACHANASSIAN. Next time, diagnose heart attack.

ILL *(laughs)*. Delicious, simply delicious.
(Claire Zachanassian turns from Doctor to inspect Gymnast, clad in shorts and vest.)

CLAIRE ZACHANASSIAN. Do another exercise.
(Gymnast bends knees, flexes arms.)
Marvellous muscles. Ever used your strength for strangling?

GYMNAST (*stiffens in consternation at knees-bend position*). For strangling?

CLAIRE ZACHANASSIAN. Now just bend your arms back again, Mister Gymnast, then forward into a press-up.

ILL (*laughs*). Clara has such a golden sense of humour! I could die laughing at one of her jokes!

DOCTOR (*still disconcerted*). I wonder. They chill me to the marrow.

ILL (*stage whisper*). She's promised us hundreds of thousands.

MAYOR (*gasps*). Hundreds of thousands?

ILL. Hundreds of thousands.

DOCTOR. God Almighty.

(*The millionairess turns away from Gymnast.*)

CLAIRE ZACHANASSIAN. And now, Mister Mayor, I'm hungry.

MAYOR. We were just waiting for your husband, my dear lady.

CLAIRE ZACHANASSIAN. You needn't. He's fishing. And I'm getting a divorce.

MAYOR. A divorce?

CLAIRE ZACHANASSIAN. Moby'll be surprised too. I'm marrying a German film star.

MAYOR. But you told us it was a very happy marriage.

CLAIRE ZACHANASSIAN. All my marriages are happy. But when I was a child I used to dream of a wedding in Guellen Cathedral. You should always fulfil your childhood dreams. It'll be a grand ceremony.

(*All sit. Claire Zachanassian takes her place between Mayor and Ill. Ill's wife beside Ill, Mayor's wife beside Mayor. Schoolmaster, Priest and Policeman at separate table, right. The four citizens, left. In background, more guests of honour, with wives. Above, the banner: 'Welcome Clärie'. Mayor stands, beaming with joy, serviette already in position, and taps on his glass.*)

MAYOR. My dear lady, fellow-citizens. Forty-five years have

33

flowed by ~~since you left our little town~~ our town founded
by ~~Crown Prince Hasso the Noble, our town so pleasantly~~
~~nestling between Konrad's Village Wood and Pückenried~~
~~Valley. Forty-five years, more than four decades, it's a~~
~~long time.~~ Many things have happened since then, many
bitter things. It has gone sadly with the world, gone sadly
with us. And yet we have never, my dear lady — our
Clarie (*applause*) — never forgotten you. Neither you, nor
your family. Your mother, that magnificent and robustly
healthy creature (*Ill whispers something to him*) tragically
and prematurely torn from our midst by tuberculosis, and
your father, that popular figure, who built the building by
the station which experts and laymen still visit so often
(*Ill whispers something to him*) — still admire so much, they
both live on in our thoughts, for they were of our best,
our worthiest. And you too, my dear lady: who, as you
gambolled through our streets — our streets, alas, so sadly
decrepit nowadays — you, a curly-headed, blonde (*Ill
whispers something to him*) — redheaded madcap, who did
not know you? Even then, everyone could sense the magic
in your personality, foresee your approaching rise to
humanity's dizzy heights. (*Takes out his notebook.*) You
were never forgotten. Literally never. Even now, the
staff at school hold up your achievements as an example
to others, and in nature studies — the most essential ones —
they were astonishing, a revelation of your sympathy for
every living creature, indeed for all things in need of
protection. And even then, people far and wide were
moved to wonder at your love of justice, at your sense of
generosity. (*Huge applause.*) For did not our Clarie obtain
food for an old widow, buying potatoes with that pocket-
money so hardly earned from neighbours, and thereby
save the old lady from dying of hunger, to mention but
one of her deeds of charity. (*Huge applause.*) My dear lady,

my dear Guelleners, that happy temperament has now developed from those tender seeds to an impressive flowering, and our redheaded madcap has become a lady whose generosity stirs the world; we need only think of her social work, of her maternity homes and her soup kitchens, of her art foundations and her children's nurseries, and now, therefore, I ask you to give three cheers for the prodigal returned: Hip, Hip, Hip, Hurrah! (*Applause.*)

(*Claire Zachanassian gets to her feet.*)

CLAIRE ZACHANASSIAN. Mister Mayor, Guelleners. I am moved by your unselfish joy in my visit. ~~As a matter of fact I was somewhat different from the child I seem to be in the Mayor's speech. When I went to school, I was thrashed. And I stole the potatoes for Widow Boll, aided by Ill, not to save the old bawd from dying of hunger, but just for once to sleep with Ill in a more comfortable bed than Konrad's Village Wood or Petersens' Barn. None the less,~~ And as my contribution to this joy of yours, I want to tell you I'm ready to give Guellen one million. Five hundred thousand for the town and five hundred thousand to be shared among each family.

(*Deathly silence.*)

MAYOR (*stammers*). One million.

(*Everyone still dumbstruck.*)

CLAIRE ZACHANASSIAN. On one condition.

(*Everyone bursts into indescribable jubilation, dancing round, standing on chairs, Gymnast performing acrobatics, etc. Ill pounds his chest enthusiastically.*)

ILL. There's Clara for you! What a jewel! She takes your breath away! Just like her, O my little sorceress!

(*Kisses her.*)

MAYOR. Madam: you said, on one condition. May I ask, on what condition?

CLAIRE ZACHANASSIAN. I'll tell you on what condition. I'm giving you a million, and I'm buying myself justice.

(*Deathly silence.*)

MAYOR. My dear lady, what do you mean by that?

CLAIRE ZACHANASSIAN. What I said.

MAYOR. Justice can't be bought.

CLAIRE ZACHANASSIAN. Everything can be bought.

MAYOR. I still don't understand.

CLAIRE ZACHANASSIAN. Boby. Step forward.

(*Butler steps forward, from right to centre, between the three tables. Takes off his dark glasses.*)

BUTLER. I don't know if any of you here still recognize me.

SCHOOLMASTER. Chief Justice Courtly.

BUTLER. Right. Chief Justice Courtly. Forty-five years ago, I was Lord Chief Justice in Guellen. I was later called to the Kaffigen Court of Appeal until, twenty-five years ago it is now, Madam Zachanassian offered me the post of Butler in her service. A somewhat unusual career, indeed, I grant you, for an academic man, however, the salary involved was really quite fantastic ...

CLAIRE ZACHANASSIAN. Get to the point, Boby.

BUTLER. As you may have gathered, Madam Claire Zachanassian is offering you the sum of one million pounds, in return for which she insists that justice be done. In other words, Madam Zachanassian will give you all a million if you right the wrong she was done in Guellen. Mr Ill, if you please.

(*Ill stands. He is pale, startled, wondering.*)

ILL. What do you want of me?

BUTLER. Step forward, Mr Ill.

ILL. Sure.

(*Steps forward, to front of table, right. Laughs uneasily. Shrugs.*)

BUTLER. The year was nineteen ten. I was Lord Chief Justice in

45 years ago

Guellen. I had a paternity claim to arbitrate. Claire Zachanassian, at the time Clara Wascher, claimed that you, Mr Ill, were her child's father.

(*Ill keeps quiet.*)

At that time, Mr Ill, you denied paternity. You called two witnesses.

ILL. Oh, it's an old story. I was young, thoughtless.

CLAIRE ZACHANASSIAN. Toby and Roby, bring in Koby and Loby.

(*The two gum-chewing giants lead pair of blind eunuchs on to centre of stage, blind pair gaily holding hands.*)

BLIND PAIR. We're on the spot, we're on the spot!

BUTLER. Do you recognize these two, Mr Ill?

(*Ill keeps quiet.*)

BLIND PAIR. We're Koby and Loby, we're Koby and Loby.

ILL. I don't know them.

BLIND PAIR. We've changed a lot, we've changed a lot!

BUTLER. Say your names.

FIRST BLIND MAN. Jacob Chicken, Jacob Chicken.

SECOND BLIND MAN. Louis Perch, Louis Perch.

BUTLER. Now, Mr Ill.

ILL. I know nothing about them.

BUTLER. Jacob Chicken and Louis Perch, do you know Mr Ill?

BLIND PAIR. We're blind, we're blind.

BUTLER. Do you know him by his voice?

BLIND PAIR. By his voice, by his voice.

BUTLER. ~~In nineteen-ten~~ (*45 years ago*) I was Judge and you the witnesses. Louis Perch and Jacob Chicken, what did you swear on oath to the Court of Guellen?

BLIND PAIR. We'd slept with Clara, we'd slept with Clara.

BUTLER. You swore it on oath, before me. Before the Court. Before God. Was it the truth?

BLIND PAIR. We swore a false oath, we swore a false oath.

BUTLER. Why, Jacob Chicken and Louis Perch?

BLIND PAIR. Ill bribed us, Ill bribed us.

BUTLER. With what did he bribe you?

BLIND PAIR. With a pint of brandy, with a pint of brandy.

CLAIRE ZACHANASSIAN. And now tell them what I did with you, Koby and Loby.

BUTLER. Tell them.

BLIND PAIR. The lady tracked us down, the lady tracked us down.

BUTLER. Correct. Claira Zachanassian tracked you down. To the ends of the earth. Jacob Chicken had emigrated to Canada and Louis Perch to Australia. But she tracked you down. And then what did she do with you?

BLIND PAIR. She gave us to Toby and Roby, she gave us to Toby and Roby.

BUTLER. And what did Toby and Roby do to you?

BLIND PAIR. Castrated and blinded us, castrated and blinded us.

BUTLER. And there you have the full story. One Judge, one accused, two false witnesses: a miscarriage of justice in the year nineteen ten. Isn't that so, plaintiff?

CLAIRE ZACHANASSIAN (*stands*). That is so.

ILL (*stamping on floor*). It's over and done with, dead and buried! It's an old, crazy story.

BUTLER. What happened to the child, plaintiff?

CLAIRE ZACHANASSIAN (*gently*). It lived one year.

BUTLER. What happened to you?

CLAIRE ZACHANASSIAN. I became a prostitute.

BUTLER. What made you one?

CLAIRE ZACHANASSIAN. The judgment of that court made me one.

BUTLER. And now you desire justice, Claire Zachanassian?

CLAIRE ZACHANASSIAN. I can afford it. A million for Guellen if someone kills Alfred Ill.

(*Deathly silence. Mrs Ill rushes to Ill, flings her arms round him.*)

MRS ILL. Freddy!

ILL. My little sorceress! You can't ask that! It was long ago. Life went on.

CLAIRE ZACHANASSIAN. Life went on, and I've forgotten nothing, Ill. Neither Konrad's Village Wood, nor Petersens' Barn; ~~neither widow Doll's bedroom~~, nor your treachery. And now we're old, the pair of us. ~~You decrepit, and me cut to bits by the surgeons' knives~~. And ~~now~~ I want accounts between us settled. You chose your life, but you forced me into mine. A moment ago you wanted time turned back, in that wood so full of the past, where we spent our young years. Well I'm turning it back now, and I want justice. Justice for a million.

(*Mayor stands, pale, dignified.*)

MAYOR. Madam Zachanassian: you forget, this is Europe. You forget, we are not savages. In the name of all citizens of Guellen, I reject your offer; and I reject it in the name of humanity. We would rather have poverty than blood on our hands.

(*Huge applause.*)

CLAIRE ZACHANASSIAN. I'll wait.

ACT TWO

The little town. (Only in outline.) In background, the Golden Apostle Hotel, exterior view. Faded 'art nouveau' architecture. Balcony. Right, a sign, 'Alfred Ill: General Store', above a grimy shop-counter backed by shelves displaying old stock. Whenever anyone enters the imaginary door, a bell rings, tinnily. Left, a sign, 'Police', above a wooden table, on it a telephone. Two chairs. It is morning. Roby and Toby, chewing gum, enter, left, bearing wreaths and flowers as at a funeral, cross stage and enter, back, the hotel. Ill at a window, watching them. His daughter on her knees scrubbing floor. His son puts a cigarette in his mouth.

ILL. Wreaths.

SON. They bring them in from the station every morning.

ILL. For the empty coffin in the Golden Apostle.

SON. It doesn't scare anyone.

ILL. The town's on my side.

    (Son lights cigarette.)

    Mother coming down for breakfast?

DAUGHTER. She's staying upstairs. Says she's tired.

ILL. You've a good mother, children. That's a fact. I just want you to know. A good mother. Let her stay upstairs, rest, save her energy. In that case, *we'll* have breakfast together. ~~It's a long time since we've done that.~~ I suggest eggs and a tin of American Ham. We'll do ourselves proud. Like in the good old days, when the Sunshine Foundry was still booming.

SON. You'll have to excuse me.

    (Stubs out cigarette.)

ILL. ~~Aren't you going to eat with us, Karl?~~

SON. I'm going to the station. There's a railwayman off sick. Maybe they want a temporary.

ILL. Railroad work in the blazing sun is no job for my boy.

SON. It's better than no job.

40

(Exit Son. Daughter stands.)

DAUGHTER. I'm going too, father.

ILL. You too? I see. May one ask my lady where?

DAUGHTER. To the Labour Exchange. They may have a vacancy.

(Exit Daughter. Ill, upset, takes out handkerchief, blows nose.)

ILL. Good kids, fine kids.

(A few bars of guitar-music twang down from balcony.)

VOICE OF CLAIRE ZACHANASSIAN. Boby, pass me my left leg.

VOICE OF BUTLER. I can't find it, Madam.

VOICE OF CLAIRE ZACHANASSIAN. On the chest of drawers behind the wedding flowers.

(Enter Man One, as first customer; he goes through imaginary door into Ill's shop.)

ILL. 'Morning, Hofbauer.

MAN ONE. Cigarettes.

ILL. Same as usual?

MAN ONE. Not those, I want the green ones.

ILL. They cost more.

MAN ONE. On account.

ILL. Since it's you, Hofbauer, and we should all stick together.

MAN ONE. That's a guitar playing.

ILL. One of those Sing Sing gangsters.

(Blind pair walk out of hotel carrying rods and other appurtenances proper to fishing.)

BLIND PAIR. Lovely morning, Alfred, lovely morning.

ILL. Go to hell.

BLIND PAIR. We're going fishing, we're going fishing.

(Exit blind pair, left.)

MAN ONE. Gone to Guellen Pond.

ILL. With her seventh husband's fishing tackle.

MAN ONE. They say he's lost his tobacco plantations.

ILL. They belong to the millionairess.

MAN ONE. The eighth wedding will be gigantic. She announced their engagement yesterday.

(Claire Zachanassian appears on balcony in background, dressed for the morning. Moves her right hand, her left leg. Sporadic notes plucked on the guitar accompany the balcony scene which follows, after the fashion of opera-recitative, pointing the text now with a waltz, now with snatches of national or traditional songs, anthems, etc.)

CLAIRE ZACHANASSIAN. I'm assembled again. Roby, the Armenian folk-song!

(Guitar music.)

Zachanassian's favourite tune. He used to love listening to it. Every morning. An exemplary man, that old tycoon. With a veritable navy of oil tankers. And racing-stables. And millions more in cash. It was worth a marriage. A great teacher, and a great dancer; a real devil. I've copied him completely.

(Two women come in, hand Ill milk-cans.)

FIRST WOMAN. Milk, Mr Ill.

SECOND WOMAN. My can, Mr Ill.

ILL. A very good morning to you. A quart of milk for the ladies.

(Opens a milk-drum, prepares to ladle milk.)

FIRST WOMAN. Jersey milk, Mr Ill.

SECOND WOMAN. Two quarts of Jersey, Mr Ill.

ILL. Jersey.

(Opens another drum, ladles milk.)

(Claire Zachanassian assesses morning critically through lorgnette.)

CLAIRE ZACHANASSIAN. A fine autumn morning. Light mist in the streets, a silvery haze, and the sky above precisely the shade of violet-blue Count Holk used to paint. My third husband. The Foreign Minister. He used to spend his holidays painting. They were hideous paintings.
(She sits, with elaborate ceremony.)
~~The Count was a hideous person.~~

FIRST WOMAN. And butter. Half a pound.

SECOND WOMAN. And super-bread. Four large loaves.

ILL. I see we've had a legacy, ladies.

THE TWO WOMEN. On account.

ILL. Share the rough and share the smooth.

FIRST WOMAN. And a bar of chocolate.

SECOND WOMAN. Two bars.

ILL. On account?

FIRST WOMAN. On account.

SECOND WOMAN. We'll eat those here, Mr Ill.

FIRST WOMAN. It's much nicer here, Mr Ill.
(They sit at back of shop eating chocolate.)

CLAIRE ZACHANASSIAN. A Winston. I will try that brand my seventh husband made, just once, now I've divorced him; poor Moby, with his fishing passion. He must be so sad sitting in the Portugal Express.
(Butler hands her a cigar, gives her a light.)

MAN ONE. Look, sitting on the balcony, puffing at her cigar.

ILL. Always some wickedly expensive brand.

MAN ONE. Sheer extravagance. She ought to be ashamed, in front of the poor.

CLAIRE ZACHANASSIAN *(smoking)*. Curious. Quite smokeable.

ILL. Her plan's misfired. I'm an old sinner, Hofbauer — who isn't. It was a mean trick I played on her when I was a kid,

43

but the way they all rejected the offer, all the Guelleners in the Golden Apostle unanimously, that was the finest moment of my life.

CLAIR ZACHANASSIAN. Boby. Whisky. Neat.

(Enter Man Two, as second customer, poor and tattered and torn, like everyone else.)

MAN TWO. 'Morning. It'll be a hot day.

MAN ONE. Very fine and warm for the time of the year.

ILL. Extraordinary custom this morning. Not a soul for as long as you like and suddenly these past few days they're flocking in.

MAN ONE. We'll stick by you. We'll stick by *our* Ill. Come what may.

THE TWO WOMEN (*munching chocolate*). Come what may, Mr Ill, come what may.

MAN TWO. Remember, you're the town's most popular personality.

MAN ONE. Our most important personality.

MAN TWO. You'll be elected Mayor in spring.

MAN ONE. It's dead certain.

THE TWO WOMEN (*munching chocolate*). Dead certain, Mr Ill, dead certain.

MAN TWO. Brandy.

(Ill reaches to shelf.)

(Butler serves whisky.)

CLAIRE ZACHANASSIAN. Wake the new guy. Can't bear my husbands sleeping all the time.

ILL. ~~Five and three.~~

MAN TWO. Not that.

ILL. It's what you always drink.

MAN TWO. Cognac.

ILL. It costs thirty-seven and nine. No one can afford that.

MAN TWO. Got to give yourself a treat sometimes.

(A half-naked girl rushes headlong over stage, pursued by Toby.)

FIRST WOMAN (munching chocolate). It's a scandal, the way Louisa behaves.

SECOND WOMAN (munching chocolate). And to make matters worse she's engaged to that blond musician in Gunpowder Street.

(Ill takes down Cognac.)

ILL. Cognac.

MAN TWO. And tobacco. For my pipe.

ILL. Tobacco.

MAN TWO. The Export.

(Ill totals account.)

(Husband VIII appears on balcony — the film star, tall, slender, red moustache, bath-robe. May be played by same actor as Husband VII.)

HUSBAND VIII. Isn't it divine, Hopsi. Our first engagement breakfast. Really a dream. A little balcony, the lime-tree rustling, the Town Hall fountain softly plashing, a few hens scampering right across the sidewalk, housewives' voices chattering away over their little daily cares and there, beyond the roof-tops, the Cathedral spires!

CLAIRE ZACHANASSIAN. Sit down, Hoby. Stop babbling. I can see the landscape. And thoughts aren't your strong point.

MAN TWO. She's sitting up there with her husband now.

FIRST WOMAN (munching chocolate). Her eighth.

SECOND WOMAN (munching chocolate). Handsome gentleman. Acts in films. My daughter saw him as the poacher in a country-life feature.

FIRST WOMAN. I saw him when he was the priest in a Graham Greene.

(Claire Zachanassian is kissed by Husband VIII. *Guitar twangs chords.)*

MAN TWO. You can get anything you want with money. *(Spits.)*

MAN ONE. Not from us. *(Bangs fist on table.)*

~~ILL. One pound three shillings and threepence.~~

MAN TWO. On account.

ILL. I'll make an exception this week; only you make sure you pay on the first, when the dole's due.

~~*(Man Two crosses to door.)*~~

ILL. Helmesberger!

(Man Two halts. Ill goes after him.)

You're wearing new shoes. New yellow shoes.

MAN TWO. So what?

(Ill stares at Man One's feet.)

ILL. You too, Hofbauer. You're wearing new shoes too.

(His gaze alights on the women; he walks slowly towards them, terror-stricken.)

You too. New shoes. New yellow shoes.

MAN ONE. What's so extraordinary about new shoes?

MAN TWO. You can't go around in the same old shoes for ever.

ILL. New shoes. How did you all get new shoes?

THE TWO WOMEN. We got them on account, Mr Ill, we got them on account.

ILL. ~~You got them on account. You got things on account from me too. Better tobacco, better milk, Cognac.~~ Why are all the shops suddenly giving you credit?

MAN TWO. You're giving us credit too.

ILL. How are you going to pay?

(Silence. He begins throwing his wares at the customers. They all run away.)

How are you going to pay? How are you going to pay? How? How?

(He rushes off, back.)

HUSBAND VIII. Township's getting rowdy.

CLAIRE ZACHANASSIAN. Village life.

HUSBAND VIII. Seems to be trouble in the shop down there.

CLAIRE ZACHANASSIAN. Haggling over the price of meat.

(Chords on guitar, fortissimo. Husband VIII leaps up, horrified.)

HUSBAND VIII. Hopsi, for heaven's sake! Did you hear that?

CLAIRE ZACHANASSIAN. The Black Panther. Spitting a little.

HUSBAND VIII *(awestruck)*. A Black Panther?

CLAIRE ZACHANASSIAN. From the Pasha of Marakeesh. A present. He's loping around in the hall. A great wicked cat with flashing eyes. I'm very fond of him.

(Policeman sits down at table, left. Drinks beer. Slow, portentous manner of speech. Ill arrives from back of stage.)

~~CLAIRE ZACHANASSIAN. You may serve, Boby.~~

~~POLICEMAN. Ill. What can I do for you? Take a seat.~~
~~(Ill remains standing.)~~
~~You're trembling.~~

ILL. I demand the arrest of Claire Zachanassian.

(Policeman thumbs tobacco into his pipe, lights it, comfortably.)

POLICEMAN. Peculiar. Highly peculiar.

~~(Butler serves breakfast, brings mail.)~~

ILL. I demand it as future Mayor.

POLICEMAN *(puffing clouds of smoke)*. We have not yet held the elections.

ILL. Arrest that woman on the spot.

POLICEMAN. What you mean is, you wish to charge this lady. It is then for the police to decide whether or not to arrest her. Has she infringed the law?

47

ILL. She's inciting the people of our town to kill me.

POLICEMAN. So now you want me to walk up to the lady and arrest her.

(*Pours himself beer.*)

CLAIRE ZACHANASSIAN. ~~The mail. One from Ike. Nehru. They send congratulations.~~

ILL. It's your duty.

~~POLICEMAN. Peculiar. Highly peculiar.~~

(*Drinks beer.*)

ILL. It's only natural. Perfectly natural.

POLICEMAN. My dear Ill, it's not as natural as all that. Now let's examine the matter soberly. The lady makes an offer of one million to the town of Guellen in exchange for your — you know what I'm talking about, of course. True, true, I was there. All this notwithstanding, no sufficient grounds are thereby constituted for the police taking action against Mrs Claire Zachanassian. We must abide by the law.

~~ILL. Incitement to murder.~~

POLICEMAN. Now listen here, Ill. We would only have a case of incitement to murder if the proposal to murder you were meant seriously. So much is obvious.

ILL. That's what I'm saying.

POLICEMAN. Exactly. Now, this proposal cannot be meant seriously, because one million is an exorbitant price, you have to admit that yourself. People offer a hundred, or maybe two hundred, for a job like that, not a penny more, you can bet your life on it. Which again proves the proposal wasn't meant seriously, and even if it had been the police couldn't take the lady seriously, because in that case she'd be mad. Get it?

ILL. Inspector. This proposal threatens *me*, whether the woman happens to be mad or not. That's only logical.

48

POLICEMAN. Illogical. You can't be threatened by a proposal, only by the execution of a proposal. Show me one genuine attempt to execute that proposal, for example one man who's been pointing a gun at you, and I'll be on the spot in a flash. ~~But no one, in point of fact, has any wish to execute the proposal; quite the contrary. That demonstration in the Golden Apostle was extremely impressive. It was a while ago now, but allow me to congratulate you.~~

> ~~(Drinks beer.)~~

~~ILL. I'm not quite so sure, Inspector.~~

POLICEMAN. Not quite so sure?

ILL. My customers are buying better milk, better bread, better cigarettes.

POLICEMAN. But you ought to be overjoyed! Business is better!

> ~~(Drinks beer.)~~

~~CLAIRE ZACHANASSIAN. Boby, buy up Dupont Shares.~~

ILL. Helmesberger's been in buying Cognac. A man who hasn't earned a cent for years and lives on Poor Relief soup.

~~POLICEMAN. I'll have a tot of that Cognac this evening. Helmesberger's invited me over.~~

> (Drinks beer.)

ILL. Everyone's wearing new shoes. New yellow shoes.

POLICEMAN. Whatever can you have against new shoes? I've got a new pair on myself.

> (Displays feet.)

ILL. You too.

~~POLICEMAN. Look.~~

~~ILL. Yellow as well.~~ And you're drinking Pilsener Beer.

POLICEMAN. Tastes good.

ILL. You always used to drink local beer.

POLICEMAN. Filthy stuff.

~~(*Radio music.*)~~

ILL. Listen.

POLICEMAN. What?

ILL. Music.

POLICEMAN. *The Merry Widow.*

ILL. A radio.

POLICEMAN. It's Hagholzer next door. He ought to keep his window shut.

(*Makes note in little notebook.*)

ILL. How did Hagholzer get a radio?

~~POLICEMAN. That's his business.~~

ILL. And you, Inspector, how are you going to pay for your Pilsener Beer and your new shoes?

POLICEMAN. That's my business.

(*Telephone on table rings. Policeman picks up receiver.*)

POLICEMAN. Guellen Police Station.

~~CLAIRE ZACHANASSIAN. Baby, telephone the Russians and tell them I accept their offer.~~

POLICEMAN. O.K., we'll see to it.

ILL. And how are my customers going to pay?

POLICEMAN. That doesn't concern the police.

(*Stands, takes rifle from back of chair.*)

ILL. But it does concern me. Because it's me they're going to pay with.

POLICEMAN. Nobody's threatening you.

(*Begins loading rifle.*)

ILL. The town's getting into debt. The greater the debt, the higher the standard of living. The higher the standard of living, the greater the need to kill me. And all that woman has to do is sit on her balcony, drink coffee, smoke cigars and wait. ~~That's all. Just wait.~~

POLICEMAN. You're imagining things.

ILL. You're all just waiting.
  (*Bangs on table.*)
POLICEMAN. ~~You've been drinking too much brandy.~~
  (~~Checks rifle.~~)
~~There. Now it's loaded.~~ Set your mind at rest. The
police are here to enforce respect for the law, to
maintain order and protect the individual. They know
their duty. If the faintest suspicion of a threat to you arises,
wheresoever it arises, from whatsoever source, the police
will step in, Mr Ill, you can rely upon it.
~~ILL (softly). Then how do you explain that gold tooth in your~~
~~mouth, Inspector?~~
~~POLICEMAN. What?~~
~~ILL. A gleaming new gold tooth.~~
POLICEMAN. Are you crazy?
  (*At this point Ill perceives the gun-barrel is now directed at
  himself, and his hands go slowly up.*)
~~I've no time to argue over your savings, man.~~ I've got
to go. That screwy millionairess has lost her little lap-
dog. The black panther. Now I have to hunt it
down.
  (*Goes towards back of stage and off.*)
ILL. It's me you're hunting down, me.

  (*Claire Zachanassian is reading a letter.*)
CLAIRE ZACHANASSIAN. He's coming, my dress-designer's
coming. My fifth husband, my best-looking man. He
still creates all my wedding-gowns. Roby, a minuet.
  (*Guitar plays a minuet.*)
HUSBAND VIII. But your fifth was a surgeon.
CLAIRE ZACHANASSIAN. My sixth.
  (~~Opens another letter.~~)
~~From the Boss of Western Railways.~~
~~HUSBAND VIII (astonished). I've not heard of that one at all.~~

CLAIRE ZACHANASSIAN. ~~My fourth. Impoverished. His shares belong to me.~~ I seduced him in Buckingham Palace.

HUSBAND VIII. But that was Lord Ishmael.

CLAIRE ZACHANASSIAN. So it was. You're right, Hoby. I forgot all about him and his castle in Yorkshire. ~~Then~~ this letter ~~must be~~ is from my second. Met him in Cairo. We kissed beneath the Sphinx. A most impressive evening.

(*Scene-change, right. The legend 'Town Hall' descends. Man Three enters, carries off shop-till and shifts counter into position as desk. Mayor enters. Puts revolver on table, sits. Ill enters, left. A construction-plan is affixed to wall.*)

ILL. I want to talk to you, Mister Mayor.

MAYOR. Take a seat.

ILL. As man to man. As your successor.

MAYOR. By all means.

(*Ill stays standing, watches revolver.*)

Mrs Zachanassian's panther has escaped. It's climbing around in the Cathedral. So it's best to be armed.

ILL. Sure.

MAYOR. I've called up all men owning weapons. We're not letting the children go to school.

ILL (*suspiciously*). Somewhat drastic measures.

MAYOR. It's big game hunting.

(*Enter Butler.*)

~~BUTLER. The World Bank President, Madam. Just flown in from New York.~~

~~CLAIRE ZACHANASSIAN. I'm not at home. Tell him to fly away again.~~

MAYOR. What's on your mind? ~~Go on, feel free, unburden yourself.~~

~~ILL (suspiciously). That's a fine brand you're smoking there.~~

~~MAYOR. A Pegasus. Virginia.~~

52

ILL. Pretty expensive.

MAYOR. Well worth the money.

ILL. Your Worship used to smoke another brand.

MAYOR. Sailor's Mates.

ILL. Cheaper.

MAYOR. Far too strong.

ILL. New tie?

MAYOR. Silk.

ILL. And I suppose you bought a pair of shoes?

MAYOR. I had some made in Kalberstadt. That's funny, how
did you know?

ILL. That's why I've come to see you.

MAYOR. Whatever's the matter with you? You look pale.
Are you sick?

ILL. I'm scared.

MAYOR. Scared?

ILL. Living standards are going up.

MAYOR. That's real news to me. I'd be glad if they were.

ILL. I demand official protection.

MAYOR. Eh! Whatever for?

ILL. Your Worship knows very well what for.

MAYOR. Don't you trust us?

ILL. There's a million on my head.

MAYOR. Apply to the police.

ILL. I've been to the police.

MAYOR. And that reassured you.

ILL. When the Police Inspector opened his mouth I saw a
gleaming new gold tooth.

MAYOR. You're forgetting you're in Guellen. A city of
Humanist traditions. Goethe spent a night here. Brahms
composed a quartet here. We owe allegiance to our lofty
heritage.

(Man Three enters, left, carrying typewriter.)

MAN. The new typewriter, Mister Mayor. A Remington.

53

MAYOR. It's to go in the office.

(*Man exits, right.*)

We've not deserved your ingratitude. If you're unable to place any trust in our community, I regret it for your sake. I didn't expect such a nihilistic attitude from you. After all, we live under the rule of law.

ILL. Then arrest that woman.

~~MAYOR. Peculiar. Highly peculiar.~~

~~ILL. The Police Inspector said that too.~~

MAYOR. God knows, the lady isn't acting so unreasonably. You did bribe two kids to commit perjury and fling a young girl into the lower depths.

ILL. None the less there were quite a few millions down in those lower depths, Mister Mayor.

(*Silence.*)

MAYOR. Let me say a few frank words to you.

ILL. I wish you would.

MAYOR. ~~As man to man, the way you wanted.~~ You haven't any moral right to demand the arrest of that lady, and furthermore there's no question of your becoming Mayor. I'm extremely sorry to have to tell you.

ILL. Officially?

MAYOR. It's an all-party directive.

ILL. I understand.

(*Crosses slowly to window, left, turns back on Mayor and stares out.*)

MAYOR. The fact that we condemn the lady's proposal does not mean we condone the crime which led to that proposal. The post of Mayor requires certain guarantees of good moral character which you can no longer furnish. You must realize that. We shall continue of course to show you the same friendship and regard as ever. That goes without saying.

(*Roby and Toby enter, left, with more wreaths and flowers,*

cross the stage and disappear into the Golden Apostle.)
The best thing is to pass over the whole affair in silence.
I've also requested the local paper not to let any of it get
into print.

(Ill turns.)

ILL. They've already begun adorning my coffin, Mister Mayor.
For me, silence is too dangerous.

MAYOR. But my dear Ili, what makes you think that? You
ought to be thankful we're spreading a cloak of forgetful-
ness over the whole nasty business.

ILL. You've already condemned me to death.

MAYOR. Mr Ill!

ILL. That plan proves it! It proves you have!

CLAIRE ZACHANASSIAN. Onassis will be coming. The Prince
and the Princess. Aga.

HUSBAND VIII. Ali?

CLAIRE ZACHANASSIAN. All the Riviera crowd.

HUSBAND VIII. Reporters?

CLAIRE ZACHANASSIAN. From all over the world. The Press
always attend when I get married. They need me, and I
need them.

(Opens another letter.)

From Count Holk.

HUSBAND VIII. Hopsi, this is our first breakfast together. Must
you really spend it reading letters from your former
husbands?

CLAIRE ZACHANASSIAN. I have to keep them under observa-
tion.

HUSBAND VIII. I have problems too.

(Rises to his feet, stares down into town.)

CLAIRE ZACHANASSIAN. Something wrong with your Porsche?

HUSBAND VIII. Small towns like this get me down. I know the
lime-tree's rustling, the birds are singing, the fountain's

plashing, but they were all doing all that half an hour ago. And nothing else is happening at all, either to the landscape or to the people, it's all a picture of deep, carefree peace and contentment and cosy comfort. No grandeur, no tragedy. Not a trace of the spiritual dedication of a great age.

(*Enter Priest, left, with a rifle slung round his shoulder. Over the table formerly occupied by Policeman he spreads a white cloth marked with a black cross. Leans rifle against wall of hotel. Sexton helps him on with soutane. Darkness.*)

PRIEST. Come in, Ill, come into the sacristy.

(*Ill comes in, left.*)

It's dark in here, dark but cool.

ILL. I don't want to bother you, Father.

PRIEST. The doors of the Church are open to all.

(*Perceives that Ill's gaze has settled on the rifle.*)

Don't be surprised at this weapon. Mrs Zachanassian's black panther is on the prowl. It's just been up in the choir-loft. Now it's in Petersens' Barn.

ILL. I need help.

PRIEST. What kind of help?

ILL. I'm scared.

PRIEST. Scared? Of whom?

ILL. People.

PRIEST. That the people will kill you, Ill?

ILL. They're hunting me as if I were a wild animal.

PRIEST. You should fear not people, but God; not death in the body, but in the soul. ~~Sexton, button the back of my soutane.~~

(*The citizens of Guellen materialize round the entire periphery of the stage; Policeman first, then Mayor, the four men, Painter, Schoolmaster, on patrol, rifles at the ready, stalking round.*)

56

ILL. My life's at stake.

PRIEST. Your eternal life.

ILL. There's a rise in the standard of living.

PRIEST. It's the spectre of your conscience rising.

ILL. The people are happy. The young girls are decking themselves out. The boys have put on bright shirts. The town's
getting ready to celebrate my murder, and I'm dying of
terror.

PRIEST. All they're doing is affirming life, that's all they're
doing, affirming life.

ILL. It's Hell.

PRIEST. You are your own Hell. ~~You are older than I am, and
you think you know people, but in the end one only
knows oneself.~~ Because you once betrayed a young girl
for money, many years ago, do you believe the people
will betray you now for money? You impute your own
nature to others. All too naturally. The cause of our fear
and our sin lies in our own hearts. ~~Once you have acknow-
ledged that, you will have conquered your torment and
acquired a weapon whereby to master it.~~

ILL. The Siemethofers have acquired a washing-machine.

~~PRIEST. Don't let that trouble you.~~

~~ILL. On credit.~~

~~PRIEST. You should rather be troubled by your soul's immor-
tality.~~

~~ILL. And the Stockers, a television set.~~

~~PRIEST.~~ Pray to God. Sexton, my bands.

(*Sexton positions bands round Priest.*)

Examine your conscience. Go the way of repentance, or
the world will relight the fires of your terror again and
again. It is the only way. No other way is open to us.

(*Silence. Men and rifles disappear. Shadows round rim of
stage. Fire bell begins clanging.*)

~~Now I must discharge my office, Ill, I have a baptism.~~

~~The Bible, Sexton, the Liturgy, the Book of Psalms~~. When little children begin to cry they must be led to safety, into the only ray of light which illumines the world.

(*A second bell begins to sound.*)

ILL. A second bell?

PRIEST. Hear it? Splendid tone. Rich and powerful. Just affirming life.

ILL (*cries out*). You too, Father! You too!

(*Priest flings himself on Ill, clings to him.*)

PRIEST. Flee! We are all weak, believers and unbelievers. Flee! The Guellen bells are tolling, tolling for treachery. Flee! Lead us not into temptation with your presence.

(*Two shots are fired. Ill sinks to ground, Priest kneels beside him.*)

Flee! Flee!

CLAIRE ZACHANASSIAN. Boby. They're shooting.

BUTLER. Yes, Madam, they are.

CLAIRE ZACHANASSIAN. What at?

BUTLER. The black panther escaped, Madam.

CLAIRE ZACHANASSIAN. Did they hit him?

BUTLER. He's dead, Madam, stretched out in front of Ill's shop.

CLAIRE ZACHANASSIAN. Poor little animal. ~~Roby, play a funeral march.~~

(*Funeral march on guitar. Balcony disappears. Bell rings. Stage set as for opening of Act One. The station. On wall, however, is a new, untorn time-table and, stuck almost anywhere, a great poster depicting brilliant yellow sun, with the legend 'Travel South'. Further along same wall, another, with the legend 'Visit the Passion Plays in Oberammergau'. Amidst buildings in background, a few cranes and a few new roof-tops. Thunderous pounding din of express train rushing*)

*through. Station-master standing on station salutes. Ill
emerges from background, one hand clutching little, old suitcase, and looks around. As if by chance, citizens of Guellen
come gradually closing in on him from all sides. Ill moves
hesitantly, stops.)*

MAYOR. Hallo, Ill.

ALL. Hallo! Hallo!

ILL *(hesitant)*. Hallo.

SCHOOLMASTER. Where are you off to with that suitcase?

ALL. Where are you off to?

ILL. To the station.

MAYOR. We'll take you there.

ALL. We'll take you there! We'll take you there!

   (More Guelleners keep arriving.)

ILL. You don't need to, you really don't. It's not worth the
   trouble.

MAYOR. Going away, Ill?

ILL. I'm going away.

POLICEMAN. Where are you going?

ILL. I don't know. First to Kalberstadt, then a bit further to —

SCHOOLMASTER. Ah! Then a bit further?

ILL. To Australia, preferably. I'll get the money somehow or
   other.

   (Walks on towards station.)

ALL. To Australia! To Australia!

MAYOR. But why?

ILL *(uneasily)*. You can't live in the same place for ever — year
  in, year out.

   *(Begins running, reaches station. The others amble over in
  his wake, surround him.)*

MAYOR. Emigrating to Australia. But that's ridiculous.

DOCTOR. The most dangerous thing you could do.

SCHOOLMASTER. One of those two little eunuchs emigrated to
  Australia.

POLICEMAN. This is the safest place for you.

ALL. The safest place, the safest place.

(All peers fearfully round like a cornered animal.)

ILL. I wrote to the Chief Constable in Kaffigen.

POLICEMAN. And?

ILL. No answer.

SCHOOLMASTER. Why are you so suspicious? It's incomprehensible.

MAYOR. No one wants to kill you.

ALL. No one, no one.

ILL. The Post Office didn't send the letter.

PAINTER. Impossible.

MAYOR. The Postmaster is a member of the Town Council.

SCHOOLMASTER. An honourable man.

ALL. An honourable man! An honourable man!

ILL. Look at this poster: 'Travel South'.

DOCTOR. What about it?

ILL. 'Visit the Passion Plays in Oberammergau'.

SCHOOLMASTER. What about it?

ILL. They're building!

MAYOR. What about it?

ILL. And you're all wearing new trousers.

MAN ONE. What about it?

ILL. You're all getting richer, you all own more!

ALL. What about it?

(Bell rings.)

SCHOOLMASTER. But you must see how fond we are of you.

MAYOR. The whole town's brought you to the station.

ALL. The whole town! The whole town!

ILL. I didn't ask you to come.

MAN TWO. We're surely allowed to come and say goodbye to you.

MAYOR. As old friends.

ALL. As old friends! As old friends!

(Noise of train. Station–master takes up flag. Guard appears, left, as after jumping down from train.)

GUARD *(with long–drawn wail)*. Guellen!

MAYOR. Here's your train.

ALL. Your train! Your train!

MAYOR. Well, have an enjoyable trip, Ill.

ALL. An enjoyable trip, an enjoyable trip!

DOCTOR. And long life and prosperity to you!

ALL. Long life and prosperity!

(The citizens of Guellen flock round Ill.)

MAYOR. It's time. Get on the Kalberstadt train, and God be with you.

POLICEMAN. And good luck in Australia!

ALL. Good luck, good luck!

(Ill stands motionless staring at his compatriots.)

ILL *(softly)*. Why are you all here?

POLICEMAN. Now what do you want?

STATION-MASTER. Take your seats please!

ILL. Why are you all crowding me?

MAYOR. We're not crowding you at all.

ILL. Let me pass.

SCHOOLMASTER. But we're letting you pass.

ALL. We're letting you pass, we're letting you pass.

ILL. Someone'll stop me.

POLICEMAN. Nonsense. All you need do is get on the train, and you'll see it's nonsense.

ILL. Get out of the way.

(No one moves. Several stand where they are, hands in pockets, and stare at him.)

MAYOR. I don't know what you're trying to do. It's up to you to go. Just get on the train.

ILL. Get out of the way!

SCHOOLMASTER. It's simply ridiculous of you to be afraid.

(Ill falls on knees.)

ILL. Why have you all come so close to me!

POLICEMAN. The man's gone mad.

ILL. You want to stop me going.

MAYOR. Go on! Get on the train!

ALL. Get on the train! Get on the train!
(*Silence.*)

ILL (*softly*). If I get on the train one of you will hold me back.

ALL (*emphatically*). No we won't! No we won't!

ILL. I know you will.

POLICEMAN. It's nearly time.

SCHOOLMASTER. My dear man, will you please get on the train.

ILL. I know, I know. Someone will hold me back, someone will hold me back.

STATION-MASTER. Stand clear!
(*Waves green flag, blows whistle. Guard assumes position to jump on train as Ill, surrounded by the citizens of Guellen, his head in his hands, collapses.*)

POLICEMAN. Look! He's collapsed!
(*Leaving Ill crumpled in collapse, all walk slowly towards back of stage and disappear.*)

ILL. I am lost!

ACT THREE

Petersens' Barn. Claire Zachanassian seated, left, immobile in sedan-chair, clad in white wedding-gown, veil, etc. Further left, a ladder. Further back, a hay-cart, an old hansom-cab, straw. Centre, small cask. Rags and mouldering sacks hang from beams. Enormous outspun spiders' webs. Enter Butler from back.

BUTLER. The Doctor and the Schoolmaster.

CLAIRE ZACHANASSIAN. Show them in.

> (*Enter Doctor and Schoolmaster, groping through the gloom. When at last they locate the millionairess, they bow. Both are clad in good, solid, very nearly fashionable bourgeois clothes.*)

DOCTOR/SCHOOLMASTER. Madam.

> (*Claire Zachanassian raises lorgnette, inspects them.*)

CLAIRE ZACHANASSIAN. You appear to be covered in dust, gentlemen.

> (*Both rub away dust with hands.*)

SCHOOLMASTER. Excuse us. We had to climb in over an old hansom-cab.

CLAIRE ZACHANASSIAN. I've retired to Petersens' Barn. I need peace and quiet. I found the wedding in Guellen Cathedral a strain. I'm not a dewy young maiden any more. You can sit on that cask.

SCHOOLMASTER. Thank you.

> (*He sits on it. Doctor remains standing.*)

CLAIRE ZACHANASSIAN. Pretty hot here. Suffocating, I'd say. Still, I love this barn, and the smell of hay and straw and axle-grease. Memories. The dung-fork. The hansom-cab. That busted hay-cart, and all the other implements. They were here when I was a child.

SCHOOLMASTER. A suggestive spot.

> (*Mops away sweat.*)

CLAIRE ZACHANASSIAN. An uplifting sermon by the Priest.

63

SCHOOLMASTER. First Corinthians, thirteen.

CLAIRE ZACHANASSIAN. And a very stout performance on your part, Professor, with the mixed choir. It sounded grand.

SCHOOLMASTER. Bach. From the Saint Matthew Passion. My head is still spinning with it all. The place was packed with High Society, Financiers, Film Stars ...

CLAIRE ZACHANASSIAN. Society went whizzing back to the Capital in its Cadillacs. For the wedding breakfast.

SCHOOLMASTER. My dear lady: we don't wish to take up more of your precious time than necessary. Your husband will be growing impatient.

CLAIRE ZACHANASSIAN. Hoby? I've sent him back to Geiselgasteig in his Porsche.

DOCTOR (*staggered*). To Geiselgasteig?

CLAIRE ZACHANASSIAN. My lawyers have already filed the divorce.

SCHOOLMASTER. But Madam, the wedding guests!

CLAIRE ZACHANASSIAN. They're used to it. It's my second-shortest marriage. Only the one with Lord Ishmael was a trifle quicker. What brings you here?

SCHOOLMASTER. We've come to discuss the Ill affair.

CLAIRE ZACHANASSIAN. O, has he died?

SCHOOLMASTER. Madam! We're still loyal to our Western principles.

CLAIRE ZACHANASSIAN. Then what do you want?

SCHOOLMASTER. The Guelleners have most, most regrettably acquired a number of new possessions.

DOCTOR. A considerable number.

(*Both mop off sweat.*)

CLAIRE ZACHANASSIAN. In debt?

SCHOOLMASTER. Hopelessly.

CLAIRE ZACHANASSIAN. In spite of your principles?

SCHOOLMASTER. We're only human.

DOCTOR. And now we must pay our debts.

CLAIRE ZACHANASSIAN. You know what you have to do.

SCHOOLMASTER (*bravely*). Madam Zachanassian. Let's be frank with each other. Put yourself in our melancholy position. For two decades, I have been sowing the Humanities' tender seeds in this poverty-stricken population, and our doctor too for two decades has been trundling around curing its rickets and consumption in his antediluvian Mercedes. ~~Why such agony of sacrifice? For the money? Hardly. Our fee is minimal. Furthermore I received and flatly rejected an offer from Kalberstadt College, just as the doctor here turned down a chair in Erlangen University. Out of pure love for our fellow-beings?~~ No, no, that would also be saying too much. No. We, and this entire little township with us, have hung on all these endless years because of a single hope: the hope that Guellen would rise again, in all its ancient grandeur, ~~and the untold wealth in our native soil be once again exploited. Oil is waiting under Pückenried Valley, and under Konrad's Village Wood there are minerals for the mining.~~ Madam, ~~we are not poor; we are merely forgotten.~~ We need credit, confidence, contracts, then our economy and culture will boom. Guellen has much to offer: the Foundry on Sunshine Square.

DOCTOR. Bockmann's.

SCHOOLMASTER. The Wagner Factory. Buy them. Revive them. And Guellen will boom. Invest a few hundred thousand, carefully, systematically. They'll produce a good return. Don't simply squander a million!

CLAIRE ZACHANASSIAN. I've two others.

~~SCHOOLMASTER.~~ *Doctor* ~~Don't condemn us to a lifelong struggle in vain.~~ We haven't come begging for alms. We've come to make a business proposition.

CLAIRE ZACHANASSIAN. Really. As business goes, it wouldn't be bad.

SCHOOLMASTER. My dear lady! I ~~knew you wouldn't leave us in the lurch.~~

CLAIRE ZACHANASSIAN. Only it can't be done. I can't buy Sunshine Square, because I own it already.

SCHOOLMASTER. *You* own it?

DOCTOR. And Bockmann's?

SCHOOLMASTER. The Wagner Factory?

CLAIRE ZACHANASSIAN. I own those too. And all the factories, Pückenried Valley, Petersens' Barn, the entire township; street by street and house by house. I had my agents buy the whole ramshackle lot and shut every business down. Your hopes were lunacy, your perseverance pointless, and your self-sacrifice foolish; your lives have been a useless waste.

(*Silence.*)

DOCTOR. What a monstrous thing.

CLAIRE ZACHANASSIAN. It was winter, long ago, when I left this little town, in a schoolgirl sailor suit and long red plaits, pregnant with only a short while to go, and the townsfolk sniggering at me. I sat in the Hamburg Express and shivered; but as I watched the silhouette of Petersens' Barn sinking away on the other side of the frost-flowers, I swore a vow to myself, I would come back again, one day. I've come back now. Now it's me imposing the conditions. Me driving the bargain. (*Calls —*) Roby and Toby, to the Golden Apostle. Husband number nine's on the way with his books and manuscripts.

(*The two giants emerge from background, lift sedan-chair.*)

SCHOOLMASTER. Madam Zachanassian! You're a woman whose love has been wounded. You make me think of a heroine from antiquity: of Medea. We feel for you, deeply; we understand; but because we do, we are inspired to prove you further: cast away those evil thoughts of revenge, don't try us till we break.

66

Help these poor, weak yet worthy people lead a slightly more dignified life. Let your feeling for humanity prevail!

CLAIRE ZACHANASSIAN. Feeling for humanity, gentlemen, is cut for the purse of an ordinary millionaire; with financial resources like mine you can afford a new world order. The world turned me into a whore. I shall turn the world into a brothel. ~~If you can't fork out when you want to dance, you have to put off dancing. You want to dance. They alone are eligible who pay. And I'm paying.~~ Guellen for a murder, a boom for a body. Come on, the pair of you, off we go!

(*She is borne away into background.*)

DOCTOR. My God. What shall we do?

SCHOOLMASTER. The dictates of our conscience, Doctor Nuesslin.

(*Ill's shop appears in foreground, right. New sign. Glittering new shop-counter, new till, costlier stock. Whenever anyone enters the imaginary door, a bell rings, magnificently. Behind shop-counter, Mrs Ill. Enter, left, Man One — a thriving butcher. Scattered bloodstains on his new apron.*)

MAN ONE. That was a ceremony. The whole of Guellen was on Cathedral Square watching it.

MRS ILL. Clarie deserves a little happiness, after all she's been through.

MAN ONE. Every bridesmaid was a film starlet. With breasts like this.

MRS ILL. They're in fashion today.

MAN ONE. And newspapermen. They'll be coming here too.

MRS ILL. We're simple people, Mr Hofbauer. They won't want anything from us.

MAN ONE. They pump everybody. Cigarettes.

MRS ILL. Green?

MAN ONE. Camels. And a bottle of aspirins. ~~Went to a party at Stocker's last night.~~

MRS ILL. On account?

MAN ONE. On account.

~~MRS ILL. How's business?~~

MAN ONE. Keeps me going.

MRS ILL. Me too. Can't grumble.

MAN ONE. I've got more staff.

MRS ILL. I'm getting someone on the first.

~~(Miss Louisa walks across stage in stylish clothes.)~~

~~MAN ONE. She's got her head full of dreams dressing up like that. She must imagine we'd murder Ill.~~

~~MRS ILL. Shameless.~~

MAN ONE. Where is he, by the way? Haven't seen him for quite a while.

MRS ILL. Upstairs.

(*Man One lights cigarette, cocks ear towards ceiling.*)

MAN ONE. Footsteps.

MRS ILL. Always walking around in his room. Has been for days.

MAN ONE. It's his bad conscience. Nasty trick he played on poor Madam Zachanassian.

MRS ILL. It's upset me terribly too.

MAN ONE. Getting a young girl in trouble. Rotten bastard. (*Speaks with decision.*) Mrs Ill, I hope your husband won't blabber when the journalists come.

MRS ILL. No really.

MAN ONE. What with his character.

MRS ILL. I have a hard time of it, Mr Hofbauer.

MAN ONE. If he tries showing up Clara, and telling lies, claiming she offered something for his death, or some such story, when it was only a figure of speech for unspeakable suffering, then we'll *have* to step in. Not because of the million. (*He spits.*) But because of public indignation. God

68

knows he's already put that sweet Madam Zachanassian through enough. (*He looks round.*) Is that a way up to the apartment?

MRS ILL. It's the only way up. Most inconvenient. But we're having another one built in the spring.

MAN ONE. I'd better just plant myself here. You can't be too sure.

(*Man One plants himself there, very upright stance, arms folded, quietly, like a warder. Enter Schoolmaster.*)

SCHOOLMASTER. Ill?

MAN ONE. Upstairs.

SCHOOLMASTER. It really isn't like me, but I need some kind of strong, alcoholic beverage.

MRS ILL. How nice of you to come and see us, Professor. We've a new Steinhäger in. Would you like to try it?

SCHOOLMASTER. A small glass.

MRS ILL. You too, Mr Hofbauer?

MAN ONE. No thanks. Still have to drive my Volkswagen into Kaffigen. There's pork to buy.

(*Mrs Ill pours a glassful. Schoolmaster drinks.*)

MRS ILL. But you're trembling, Professor.

SCHOOLMASTER. I've been over-drinking lately.

MRS ILL. One more won't harm.

SCHOOLMASTER. Is that him walking about?

(*Cocks ear towards ceiling.*)

MRS ILL. Up and down, all the time.

MAN ONE. God will punish him.

(*Enter, left, Painter with picture under arm. New corduroys, colourful neckerchief, black beret.*)

PAINTER. Watch out. Two reporters asked me about this shop.

MAN ONE. Suspicious.

PAINTER. I acted ignorant.

MAN ONE. Clever.

PAINTER. For you, Mrs Ill. Fresh off the easel. It's still damp.

(*Exhibits picture. Schoolmaster pours himself another drink.*)

MRS ILL. It's my husband.

PAINTER. Art's beginning to boom in Guellen. How's that for painting, eh?

MRS ILL. A real likeness.

PAINTER. Oils. Last for ever.

MRS ILL. We could hang it in the bedroom. Over the bed. Alfred'll be old one day. And you never know what might happen, it's a comfort to have a souvenir.

(*The two women from Act Two, passing by outside stop and examine wares in imaginary shop-window. Both elegantly dressed.*)

MAN ONE. Look at those women. Going to the films in broad daylight. The way they behave, you'd think we were sheer murderers!

MRS ILL. Expensive?

PAINTER. Thirty pounds.

MRS ILL. I can't pay now.

PAINTER. Doesn't matter. I'll wait, Mrs Ill, I'll be happy to wait.

SCHOOLMASTER. Those footsteps, those footsteps all the time.

(*Enter Man Two, left.*)

MAN TWO. The Press.

MAN ONE. All stick together. It's life or death.

PAINTER. Watch out he doesn't come down.

MAN ONE. That's taken care of.

(*The Guelleners gather to right. Schoolmaster having now drunk half the bottle remains standing at counter. Enter two Reporters carrying cameras.*)

FIRST REPORTER. 'Evening, folks.

GUELLENERS. How do you do.

FIRST REPORTER. Question one: How do you all feel, on the whole?

MAN ONE (*uneasily*). We're very happy of course about Madam Zachanassian's visit.

PAINTER. Moved.

MAN TWO. Proud.

FIRST REPORTER. Proud.

SECOND REPORTER. Question two for the lady behind the counter: the story goes, you were the lucky woman instead of Madam Zachanassian.

(*Silence. Guelleners manifestly shocked.*)

MRS ILL. Where did you get that story?

(*Silence. Both Reporters write impassively in notebooks.*)

FIRST REPORTER. Madam Zachanassian's two fat blind little mannikins.

(*Silence.*)

MRS ILL (*hesitant*). What did the mannikins tell you?

SECOND REPORTER. Everything.

PAINTER. Goddam.

(*Silence.*)

SECOND REPORTER. Forty years ago Claire Zachanassian and the proprietor of this shop nearly married. Right?

MRS ILL. That's right.

SECOND REPORTER. Is Mr Ill here?

MRS ILL. He's in Kalberstadt.

ALL. He's in Kalberstadt.

FIRST REPORTER. We can imagine the Ro-mance. Mr Ill and Claire Zachanassian grow up together, maybe they're next-door kids, they go to school together, go for walks in the wood, share the first kisses, they're like brother and sister, and so it goes on till Mr Ill meets you, lady, and you're the new woman, his mystery, his passion.

MRS ILL. Passion. Yes, that's how it happened, just the way you said.

FIRST REPORTER. Foxy, foxy, Mrs Ill. Claire Zachanassian grasps the situation, in her quiet, noble fashion she renounces her claims, and you marry ...

MRS ILL. For love.

GUELLENERS (*on whom light dawns*). For love.

FIRST REPORTER. For love.

(*Enter, right, Roby leading the pair of eunuchs by their ears.*)

THE PAIR (*wailing*). We won't tell any more stories, we won't tell any more stories.

(*They are dragged towards back of stage, where Toby awaits them with whip.*)

SECOND REPORTER. About your husband, Mrs Ill, doesn't he now and then, I mean, it'd be only human for him, now and then, to feel a few regrets.

MRS ILL. Money alone makes no one happy.

SECOND REPORTER (*writing*). No one happy.

FIRST REPORTER. That's a truth we in this modern world ought to write up in the sky of our hearts.

(*Enter Son, left, wearing suede jacket.*)

MRS ILL. Our son Karl.

FIRST REPORTER. Splendid youngster.

SECOND REPORTER. Is he in the know about the relationship ...

MRS ILL. There are no secrets in our family. What we always say is, anything God knows our children ought to know.

SECOND REPORTER (*writing*). Children ought to know.

(*Daughter walks into shop, wearing tennis-outfit, carrying tennis-racket.*)

MRS ILL. Our daughter Ottilie.

SECOND REPORTER. Charming.

(*Schoolmaster now calls up courage.*)

SCHOOLMASTER. Guelleners. I am your old schoolmaster. I've been quietly drinking my Steinhäger and keeping my thoughts to myself. But now I want to make a speech. I want to talk about the old lady's visit to Guellen.

(*Scrambles on to the little cask left over from the scene in Petersens' Barn.*)

MAN ONE. Have you gone mad?

MAN TWO. Stop him!

SCHOOLMASTER. Guelleners! I want to reveal the truth, even if our poverty endures for ever!

MRS ILL. You're drunk, Professor, you ought to be ashamed of yourself!

SCHOOLMASTER. Ashamed? You're the one to be ashamed, woman! You're paving your way to betray your own husband!

SON. Shut your trap!

MAN ONE. Drag him down!

MAN TWO. Kick him out!

SCHOOLMASTER. You've nearly contrived your doom!

DAUGHTER (*supplicating*). Please, Professor!

SCHOOLMASTER. Child, you disappoint me. It was up to you to speak out, and now your old schoolmaster must unleash the voice of thunder!

(*Painter breaks painting over his head.*)

PAINTER. There! You'll sabotage all my commissions!

SCHOOLMASTER. I protest! I wish to make a public appeal to world opinion! Guellen is planning a monstrous deed!

(*The Guelleners launch themselves at him as, simultaneously, in an old tatterdemalion suit, Ill enters, right.*)

ILL. Just what is going on here, in my shop!

(*The Guelleners fall back from Schoolmaster to stare at Ill, shocked. Deathly silence.*)

Professor! What are you up to on that cask!

(*Schoolmaster beams at Ill in happy relief.*)

SCHOOLMASTER. The truth, Ill. I'm telling the gentlemen of the Press the truth. Like an archangel I'm telling them, in forceful ringing tones. (*Wavers.*) Because I'm a humanist, a lover of the ancient Greeks, an admirer of Plato.

73

ILL. Hold your peace.

SCHOOLMASTER. Eh?

ILL. Get down.

SCHOOLMASTER. But humanitarianism —

ILL. Sit down.

(*Silence.*)

SCHOOLMASTER (*sobered*). Humanitarianism has to sit down. By all means — if you're going to betray truth as well.

(*Steps down from cask, sits on it, picture still round his neck.*)

ILL. Excuse this. The man's drunk.

FIRST REPORTER. Mr Ill?

ILL. What is it?

FIRST REPORTER. We're very glad we finally got to meet you. We need a few pictures. May we? (*Glances round.*) Groceries, household wares, ironmongery — I've got it: we'll take you selling an axe.

ILL (*hesitant*). An axe?

FIRST REPORTER. To the butcher. You gotta have Realism for a punch. Give me that homicidal weapon here. Your client takes the axe, weighs it in his hand, he puts an appraising expression on his face, while you lean across the counter, you're discussing it with him. O.K., let's go.

(*He arranges the shot.*)

More natural, folks, more relaxed.

(*Reporters click their cameras.*)

That's fine, just fine.

SECOND REPORTER. Now if you don't mind please, one arm round your good wife's shoulders. Son on the left, daughter on the right. That's fine. O.K., now, you're radiant with happiness, please, just brimming over with it, radiant, radiant and contented deep down inside, quietly, happily radiant.

FIRST REPORTER. Great, great, that sure was radiant.

(*Several Photographers come running in, downstage left,
cross the boards and go running out, upstage left. One photographer bawls into shop —*)

PHOTOGRAPHER. Zachanassian's got a new one. They're taking
a walk in Konrad's Village Wood, right now.

SECOND REPORTER. A new one!

FIRST REPORTER. That's good for a cover on *Life* magazine.

(*The two Reporters race out of shop. Silence. Man One is
left still gripping axe.*)

MAN ONE (*relieved*). That was a bit of luck.

PAINTER. Forgive us, Professor. If we still hope' to settle this
affair amicably, we've got to exclude the Press. Agreed?

(*Exit, followed by Man Two. But passing Ill, Man Two
pauses.*)

MAN TWO. Smart. Very smart you didn't shoot your mouth.
No one would believe a word a bastard like you said
anyway.

(*Exit Man Two.*)

~~MAN ONE. We'll be in the illustrateds, Ill.~~

~~ILL. Yes.~~

~~MAN ONE. We'll be famous.~~

~~ILL. In a manner of speaking.~~

~~MAN ONE. A Gesena.~~

~~ILL. Certainly.~~

~~MAN ONE. On account.~~

~~ILL. Of course.~~

MAN ONE. Let's face it: what you did to little Clara was a real
worm's trick.

(*Begins to go.*)

ILL. Hofbauer. The axe.

(*Man One hesitates, then returns axe to Ill. Silence in shop.
Schoolmaster is still sitting on his cask.*)

SCHOOLMASTER. I apologize. I've been trying the Steinhäger.
Must have had two or three.

ILL. It's all right.

> (*The family cross to right, and exit.*)

SCHOOLMASTER. I wanted to help you. But they shouted me down, and you didn't want my help either. (*Disengages himself from picture.*) Ah, Ill. What kind of people are we. That infamous million is burning up our hearts. Pull yourself together, fight for your life. Enlist the sympathy of the Press. You haven't any more time to lose.

ILL. I'm not fighting any more.

SCHOOLMASTER (*amazed*). Tell me, has fear driven you completely out of your senses?

ILL. I've realized I haven't the least right on my side.

SCHOOLMASTER. No right? No right compared to that damned old woman, that brazen arch-whore changing husbands while we watch, and making a collection of our souls?

ILL. That's all my fault, really.

SCHOOLMASTER. Your fault?

ILL. I made Clara what she is, and I made myself what I am, a failing shopkeeper with a bad name. What shall I do, Schoolmaster? Play innocent? It's all my own work, the Eunuchs, the Butler, the coffin, the million. I can't help myself and I can't help any of you, any more.

> (*Takes up torn painting and examines it.*)

My portrait.

SCHOOLMASTER. Your wife wanted to hang it in your bedroom. Over the bed.

ILL. Kuhn will paint another.

> (*Lays picture down on counter. Schoolmaster stands with an effort, sways.*)

SCHOOLMASTER. I'm sober. All at once.

> (*He reels across to Ill.*)

You are right. Absolutely. It's all your fault. And now I want to tell you something, Alfred Ill, something fundamental.

(Stands facing Ill, stiff as a ramrod and hardly swaying at all.)

They will kill you. I've known it from the beginning, and you've known it too for a long time, even if no one else in Guellen wants to admit it. The temptation is too great and our poverty is too wretched. But I know something else. I shall take part in it. I can feel myself slowly becoming a murderer. My faith in humanity is powerless to stop it. And because I know all this, I have also become a sot. I too am scared, Ill, just as you have been scared. And finally I know that one day an old lady will come for us too, and then what happened to you will also happen to us, but soon, perhaps in a few hours, I shall have lost that knowledge. *(Silence.)* Another bottle of Steinhäger.

(Ill gets him a bottle, Schoolmaster hesitates, then firmly takes and clutches bottle.)

Put it on my account.

(Walks slowly out.

The family return. Ill looks round at his shop as if dreaming.)

ILL. It's all new. Our place looks so modern nowadays. Clean. Inviting. I've always dreamed of having a shop like this.

(Takes Daughter's tennis-racket from her hand.)

~~D'you play tennis?~~

~~DAUGHTER. I've had a couple of lessons.~~

~~ILL. Early mornings, eh? Instead of going to the Labour Exchange?~~

~~DAUGHTER. All my friends play tennis.~~

(Silence.)

ILL. I was looking out of my bedroom window, Karl, and I saw you in an automobile.

SON. It's only an Opel, they aren't so expensive.

~~ILL. When did you learn to drive?~~

(Silence.)

77

~~Instead of looking for work on the railroad in the blazing sun, eh?~~

SON. Sometimes.

(Son, embarrassed, crosses to cask on which the drunk has been sitting, shoves it to right and out.)

ILL. I was looking for my Sunday suit. I found a fur coat hanging beside it.

MRS ILL. It's on approval.

(Silence.)

Everyone's making debts, Freddy. You're the only one throwing fits of hysterics. It's simply ridiculous of you to be scared. It's so obvious the thing's going to be settled peacefully, without anyone harming a hair of your head. Clarie won't go the whole way, I know her, she's too good-hearted.

DAUGHTER. Of course, father.

SON. Surely you realize that.

(Silence.)

ILL *(slowly)*. It's Saturday, Karl, I'd like to go for a drive in your automobile, just once. In our automobile.

SON *(uncertainly)*. You'd like that?

ILL. Put on your best clothes. We'll all go for a drive together.

MRS ILL *(uncertainly)*. Am I to go with you? But surely that wouldn't do.

ILL. And why wouldn't it do? Go and put on your fur coat, this'll be an opportunity to christen it. I'll be seeing to the till in the meantime.

(Exit Mother and Daughter, right. Exit Son, left. Ill busies himself at till. Enter, left, Mayor carrying rifle.)

MAYOR. Good evening, Ill. Don't let me trouble you. I'll just have a quick look round.

ILL. By all means.

(Silence.)

MAYOR. Brought you a gun.

ILL. Thanks.

MAYOR. It's loaded.

ILL. I don't need it.

(*Mayor leans gun against counter.*)

MAYOR. There's a public meeting this evening. In the Golden Apostle. In the auditorium.

ILL. I'll be there.

MAYOR. Everyone'll be there. We're dealing with your case. We're under a certain amount of pressure.

ILL. That's what I feel.

MAYOR. The motion will be rejected.

ILL. Possibly.

MAYOR. People make mistakes, of course.

ILL. Of course.

(*Silence.*)

MAYOR (*cautiously*). In such a case, Ill, would you then submit to the judgment? Since the Press will be present.

ILL. The Press?

MAYOR. And the Radio. And the Television and News-reel cameras. Very ticklish situation. Not only for you. For us too, believe you me. We're famous as the old lady's native town, and also because of her marriage in the Cathedral here. So now they're going to run a commentary on our ancient democratic institutions.

(*Ill busies himself at till.*)

ILL. Are you making public knowledge of the lady's offer?

MAYOR. Not directly. Only the initiated will grasp the full meaning of the procedure.

ILL. The fact that my life is at stake.

(*Silence.*)

MAYOR. I've let a few hints leak out to the Press that Madam Zachanassian may — there's just a possibility she may make an endowment and that you, Ill, as her childhood friend, will have negotiated that endowment. Of course, it's well

known by now that you in fact were her childhood friend.
This means that so far as appearances go, you'll have an
absolutely clean record.

ILL. That's kind of you.

MAYOR. To be quite frank, I didn't do it for your sake. I was
really thinking of your fine, upright, honest family.

ILL. I see.

MAYOR. You've got to admit we're playing fair with you.
Up to now, you've kept quiet. Good. But will you go on
keeping quiet? If you intend to talk, we'll have to settle
the whole business without a public meeting.

ILL. I understand.

MAYOR. Well?

ILL. I'm glad to hear an open threat.

MAYOR. I'm not threatening you, Ill, you're threatening us.
If you talk, we'll have to act accordingly. First.

ILL. I'll keep quiet.

MAYOR. However the decision turns out at the meeting?

ILL. I'll accept it.

MAYOR. Good.

(Silence.)

I'm glad you'll abide by the ruling of our community
court, Ill. You still have a certain glimmer of honour in
you. But wouldn't it be better if we didn't even have to
call on that community court to assemble?

ILL. What are you trying to say?

MAYOR. When I came in, you said you didn't need the gun.
But now, perhaps, you do need it.

(Silence.)

We might then tell the lady we had brought you to
justice and that way, just the same, receive the money.
You can imagine the sleepless nights I've spent on that
suggestion. But isn't it your duty, as a man of honour, to
draw your own conclusions and make an end of your

life? If only out of public spirit, and your love for your
native town. ~~You're well aware of our wretched priva-~~
~~tions, the misery here, and the hungry children ...~~
~~ILL. You're all doing very well~~
~~MAYOR. Ill!~~

ILL. Mister Mayor! I have been through a Hell. I've watched
you all getting into debt, and I've felt death creeping
towards me, nearer and nearer with every sign of prosperity. If you had spared me that anguish, that gruesome
terror, it might all have been different, this discussion
might have been different, and I might have taken the
gun. For all your sakes. Instead, I shut myself in. I conquered my fear. Alone. It was hard, and now it's done.
There is no turning back. You *must* judge me, now. I shall
accept your judgment, whatever it may be. For me, it
will be justice; what it will be for you, I do not know.
God grant you find your judgment justified. You may
kill me, I will not complain and I will not protest, nor
will I defend myself. But I cannot spare you the task of
the trial.

    (*Mayor takes back gun.*)

MAYOR. Pity. You're missing a chance to redeem yourself and
be a more or less decent human being. I might have known
it was too much to ask you.

~~ILL. Match, Mister Mayor.~~

    ~~(Lights cigarette for Mayor.~~ *Exit Mayor.*
    Enter Mrs Ill in fur coat, Daughter in red dress.)
You look very distinguished, Matilda.

MRS ILL. Persian lamb.

ILL. Like a real lady.

MRS ILL. Quite expensive.

ILL. Pretty dress, Ottilie. But isn't it a little bold?

DAUGHTEr. O silly Daddy. You should just take a peek at my
evening dress.

(Shop disappears. Son drives up in motor-car.)

ILL. Fine automobile. You know, I toiled a lifetime to get a little property, a mite of comfort, say for example an automobile like this, and now, my time's up, but still, I'd like to know how it feels to be inside one of these. Matilda, get in the back with me, you in the front, Ottilie, next to Karl.

(They get into motor-car.)

SON. It'll do eighty.

ILL. Not so fast. I want to see a bit of the scenery, a bit of the town, I've lived here nearly seventy years. They've cleaned up the old streets. Lot of reconstruction, already. Grey smoke, coming out of those chimneys. Geraniums there in the window-boxes. Sunflowers. The Goethe Arch, they've planted roses in the gardens. Don't the children look happy; and sweethearts, all over the place. Brahms Square, that's a new apartment block.

MRS ILL. They're re-doing the Café Hodel.

DAUGHTER. There goes the Doctor, in his Mercedes 300.

ILL. Look at the plain, and the light on the hills beyond, all golden, today. Impressive, when you go into the shadows and then out again into the light. Those cranes on the horizon by the Wagner Factory look like giants; and the Bockmann chimneys too.

SON. They're starting up again.

ILL. What's that?

SON *(louder)*. They're starting up again.

(Hoots horn.)

MRS ILL. Funny little car.

SON. Bubble-car: Messerschmidt. Every kid in the Technical College has one.

DAUGHTER. C'est terrible.

MRS ILL. Ottilie's taking her Advanced in French and German.

ILL. Useful. Sunshine Square. The Foundry. Long time since
I've been out here.

SON. They're going to build a bigger one.

ILL. You'll have to talk louder at this speed.

SON (*louder*). They're going to build a bigger one. Stocker
again, who else. Passing everybody in his Buick.

DAUGHTER. Un nouveau riche.

ILL. Now drive through Pückenried Valley. Go past the
Moor and down Poplar Boulevard, round Prince Hasso's
Hunting Lodge. Colossal clouds in the sky, banks of them,
real summer-time castles. It's a beautiful country in a soft
twilight. I feel I'm seeing it today the first time.

DAUGHTER. Atmosphere like Tennyson.

ILL. Like what?

MRS ILL. Ottilie's studying literature too.

ILL. It'll give her advantages.

SON. Hofbauer in his Volkswagen. Coming back from Kaffigen.

DAUGHTER. With the pork.

MRS ILL. Karl drives well. Very smart, the way he cut that
corner. You don't feel frightened with him.

SON. First gear. The road's getting steep.

ILL. I always used to get out of breath walking up here.

MRS ILL. I'm so glad I brought my fur coat. It's getting quite
chilly.

ILL. You've come the wrong way. This road goes to Beisenbach. You'll have to go back and then left, into Konrad's
Village Wood.

   (*Motor-car reverses into background. Enter, carrying wooden
   bench, and wearing dress-suits now, the four citizens who
   designate trees.*)

MAN ONE.
We're standing in for trees again,
A spruce, a fir, a beech, a pine,

83

MAN TWO.
We're bird and beast, we're timid deer,
We're woodpeckers;
MAN THREE.
The cuckoos here
Sing songs of bygone nights and dawns,
MAN FOUR.
Outraged today by motor horns.

SON (*hoots horn*). Another deer. That animal just won't get off the road.
    (*Man Three jumps off the road.*)
DAUGHTER. They're so trusting. The poaching's stopped.
ILL. Stop under these trees.
SON. Sure.
MRS ILL. What do you want to do?
ILL. Walk through the woods. (*He gets out.*) The Guellen bells are ringing. They sound so good from here. Time to stop work.
SON. Four of them. First time they sound like real bells.
ILL. Everything's yellow. The autumn's really here. The leaves on the ground are like layers of gold.
    (*He tramples amongst leaves on the ground.*)
SON. We'll wait for you down by Guellen Bridge.
ILL. You needn't wait. I shall walk through the wood into town. To the public meeting.
MRS ILL. In that case we'll drive into Kalberstadt, Freddy, and see a film.
SON. 'Bye, father.
DAUGHTER. Au revoir, papa.
MRS ILL. See you soon! See you soon!
    (*Motor-car with family in it disappears, returns in reverse, the family waving; Ill watches them out of sight. Sits on wooden bench, left.*

84

Rush of wind. Enter Roby and Toby, right, bearing sedan-chair in which Claire Zachanassian, seated, wearing her customary clothes. Roby carries guitar slung at his back. Husband IX comes striding in beside her — the Nobel Prize-winner, tall, slender, hair peppered grey, moustache. (May also be played by same actor as earlier husbands.) Butler brings up rear.)

CLAIRE ZACHANASSIAN. It's the Konrad's Village Wood. Roby and Toby, stop a moment.

(Claire Zachanassian descends from sedan-chair, inspects wood through lorgnette, and strokes back of Man One.)

Bark-beetle. This tree's withering away. *(Notices Ill.)* Alfred! How nice to see you! ~~I'm visiting my Wood.~~

ILL. ~~Does Konrad's Village Wood belong to you as well?~~

CLAIRE ZACHANASSIAN. ~~Yes, it does.~~ May I sit down beside you?

ILL. By all means. I've just said goodbye to my family. They've gone to the cinema. Karl's got himself an automobile.

CLAIRE ZACHANASSIAN. Progress.

(Sits down beside Ill, right.)

ILL. ~~Ottilie's taking a course in literature. French and German as well.~~

CLAIRE ZACHANASSIAN. ~~You see, they have developed a sense of ideals after all.~~ Zoby, come and make your bow. My ninth husband. Nobel Prize-winner.

ILL. Very glad to meet you.

CLAIRE ZACHANASSIAN. He's particularly interesting when he stops thinking. Stop thinking a moment, Zoby.

HUSBAND IX. But Precious ...

CLAIRE ZACHANASSIAN. No showing off.

HUSBAND IX. Oh all right.

(Stops thinking.)

85

CLAIRE ZACHANASSIAN. See? Now he looks like a diplomat. Reminds me of Count Holk, except that he couldn't write books. He wants to go into retirement, publish his memoirs and manage my property.

ILL. Congratulations.

CLAIRE ZACHANASSIAN. I feel uneasy about it. You only have husbands for display purposes, they shouldn't be useful. Zoby, go away and do some research. You'll find the historical ruins on the left.

(*Husband* IX *goes away to do some research. Ill glances round.*)

ILL. What's happened to the two Eunuchs?

CLAIRE ZACHANASSIAN. They were getting garrulous. I had them shipped off to Hong Kong. Put in one of my opium dens. They can smoke and they can dream. The Butler will follow them soon. I shan't be needing him either, any more. Boby, a Romeo and Juliet.

(*Butler emerges from background, passes her a cigarette case.*)

Would you like one, Alfred?

ILL. Thank you.

CLAIRE ZACHANASSIAN. Here, then. Give us a light, Boby.

(*They smoke.*)

ILL. Smells good.

CLAIRE ZACHANASSIAN. We often smoked together in this wood; do you remember? You used to buy the cigarettes from little Matilda. Or steal them.

(*Man One taps key on pipe.*)

That woodpecker again.

MAN FOUR. Cuckoo! Cuckoo!

CLAIRE ZACHANASSIAN. Would you like Roby to play for you on his guitar?

ILL. Please.

CLAIRE ZACHANASSIAN. My amnestied killer plays well. I need

him for meditative moments. I hate gramophones. And radios.

ILL. There's an army marching in an African valley.

CLAIRE ZACHANASSIAN. Your favourite song. I taught it to him.

(*Silence. They smoke. Cuckoo call, forest sounds, etc. Roby plays ballad.*)

ILL. You had – I mean, we had a child.

CLAIRE ZACHANASSIAN. True.

ILL. Was it a boy or a girl?

CLAIRE ZACHANASSIAN. A girl.

ILL. And what name did you give it?

CLAIRE ZACHANASSIAN. Genevieve.

ILL. Pretty name.

CLAIRE ZACHANASSIAN. I only saw the thing once. At birth. Then they took it away. The Salvation Army.

ILL. Eyes?

CLAIRE ZACHANASSIAN. Not yet open.

ILL. Hair?

CLAIRE ZACHANASSIAN. I think it had black hair. But then new-born babies often have black hair.

ILL. Yes, they often do.

(*Silence. They smoke. Guitar plays.*)

Where did it die?

CLAIRE ZACHANASSIAN. With some people. I've forgotten their name.

ILL. What of?

CLAIRE ZACHANASSIAN. Meningitis. Perhaps it was something else. I did receive a card from the authorities.

ILL. In cases of death you can rely on them.

(*Silence.*)

CLAIRE ZACHANASSIAN. I've talked about our little girl. Now you talk about me.

ILL. About you?

CLAIRE ZACHANASSIAN. The way I was, when I was seventeen, when you loved me.

ILL. I had to look for you a long while once in Petersens' Barn; I found you in the old carriage with nothing on but a blouse and a long straw between your lips.

CLAIRE ZACHANASSIAN. You were strong and brave. You fought that railwayman when he tried to paw me. I wiped the blood off your face with my red petticoat.

(Guitar stops playing.)

The ballad has ended.

ILL. One more: 'Home Sweet Home'.

CLAIRE ZACHANASSIAN. Yes, Roby can play that.

(Guitar resumes play.)

ILL. Thank you for the wreaths, and for the chrysanthemums and roses. They'll look fine on the coffin in the Golden Apostle. Distinguished. They fill two rooms already. Now the time has come. It is the last time we shall sit in our old wood and hear the cuckoo calling and the sound of the wind. They are meeting this evening. They will sentence me to death, and one of them will kill me. I don't know who it will be, and I don't know where it will happen, I only know that my meaningless life will end.

CLAIRE ZACHANASSIAN. I shall take you in your coffin to Capri. I have had a mausoleum built, in my Palace Park. It is surrounded by cypress-trees. Overlooking the Mediterranean.

ILL. I only know it from pictures.

CLAIRE ZACHANASSIAN. Deep blue. A grandiose panorama. You will remain there. A dead man beside a stone idol. Your love died many years ago. But my love could not die. Neither could it live. It grew into an evil thing, like me, like the pallid mushrooms in this wood, and the blind, twisted features of the roots, all overgrown by my golden millions. Their tentacles sought you out, to take your life, because your life belonged to me, for ever. You are in their toils now, and you are lost. You will soon be no more than a dead love in my memory, a gentle ghost haunting the wreckage of a house.

ILL. 'Home Sweet Home' has ended now as well.

(*Husband* IX *returns.*)

CLAIRE ZACHANASSIAN. Here's the Nobel Prize-winner. Back from his ruins. Well, Zoby?

HUSBAND IX. Early Christian. Sacked by the Huns.

CLAIRE ZACHANASSIAN. What a pity. Give me your arm. Roby, Toby, the sedan.

(*Gets into sedan-chair.*)

Goodbye, Alfred.

ILL. Goodbye, Clara.

(*The sedan-chair is borne away to background. Ill remains seated on bench. The trees put away their twigs. Portal descends, with usual curtains and draperies, also inscription:* LIFE IS SERIOUS, ART SERENE. *Policeman emerges from background, in swashbuckling new uniform, sits beside Ill. A Radio Commentator enters, begins talking into microphone while the Guelleners assemble. Everyone in new evening gowns and dress-suits. Hordes of Press Photographers, Reporters, Cameramen.*)

RADIO COMMENTATOR. Ladies and gentlemen: Radio Newsreel has been bringing you a Scene from the Birthplace and a Conversation with the Priest, and now it's time to go over to the Public Meeting. We're nearing the climax of this visit which Madam Claire Zachanassian has kindly accorded to her charming, friendly little home-town. ~~Of course it's unfortunate the famous lady won't be putting in a personal appearance; on the other hand we will be hearing the Mayor, because he's slated to make an important announcement in her name.~~ Right now we're coming

to you from the auditorium of the Golden Apostle, an
hotel which can boast of a bed where Goethe once spent
the night. ~~And now the townsmen are assembling on the~~
~~stage, in less exciting days the scene of local club gatherings~~
~~and guest shows by the Kalberstadt Repertory Players.~~
~~The Mayor's just informed me this is an old custom. The~~
~~women are all down in the auditorium --~~ it seems this is
an old custom too. I can't tell you what a solemn atmosphere it is, the tension's really extraordinary. All the news-
reel cameras are here, I can see my colleagues from T.V.,
there are reporters from all over the world, and now here
comes the Mayor and he's going to begin his speech, we're
crossing over to him now!

(*Radio Commentator crosses over to Mayor, who is standing in
centre of stage, round him in a semi-circle the men of Guellen.*)

MAYOR. Ladies and gentlemen, Citizens of Guellen. I'm very
happy to welcome you all here this evening. I declare this
meeting open. We have one, single item on our agenda.
It is my privilege to announce that Madam Claire
Zachanassian, ~~daughter of our worthy fellow-citizen~~
~~Godfrey Wascher -- the architect -- intends~~ to make us a
donation of one million pounds.

(*Whispers among the Press.*)

Five hundred thousand for the town and five hundred
thousand to be shared among all citizens.

(*Silence.*)

RADIO COMMENTATOR (*subdued*). What a sensation, listeners,
what a colossal sensation. One endowment, and every
inhabitant of this little town has suddenly become a well-
to-do citizen. It must constitute one of the greatest social
experiments of the age. The public here are gasping for
breath, there's a deathly silence, O, they're awestruck, you
can see it on every face.

MAYOR. I leave the floor to the Headmaster of our College.

(Radio Commentator crosses with microphone to School-master.)

SCHOOLMASTER. Guelleners: I want to raise one point we must all clearly understand – namely, in making her donation, Madam Claire Zachanassian has a definite aim. ~~What is her aim? Is it her aim to make us happy with money? Is it merely her aim to heap gold on our heads? To revive the Wagner Factory and Bockmann's and the Foundry on Sunshine Square? You know very well it is not.~~ Madam Claire Zachanassian has a more important aim. Her aim is to have the spirit of this community transformed – transformed to the spirit of justice. We, staggered by this demand, ask: have we not always been a just community?

VOICE ONE. Never!

VOICE TWO. We fostered a crime!

VOICE THREE. A false judgment!

VOICE FOUR. A perjury!

WOMAN'S VOICE. A villain!

OTHER VOICES. Hear! Hear!

SCHOOLMASTER. O people of Guellen! Such is the bitter truth! We have connived at injustice! I am of course fully aware of the material possibilities inherent for all of us in a million. Nor am I blind to the fact that poverty is the root of much evil, nay, of great hardship. And yet, and yet: we are not moved by the money *(huge applause)*: we are not moved by ambitious thoughts of prosperity and good living, and luxury: we are moved by this matter of justice, and the problem of how to apply it. Nor yet by justice alone, but also by all those ideals, for which our forebears lived and fought, and for which they died; and which constitute the values of our Western World. *(Huge applause.)* When individual persons slight the ideal of brotherly love, disobey the commandment to succour the weak, spurn the marriage vow, deceive the courts and plunge young mothers into misery, then Freedom is at stake. (*Catcalls.*) Now, in God's name, we must take our ideals seriously, even unto death. (*Huge applause.*) For what would be the sense of wealth, which created not a wealth of grace? Yet grace can only be accorded those who hunger after grace. People of Guellen, do you have that hunger? Or is all your hunger common hunger, physical and profane? That is the question. As Head of your College, I put it to you all. Only if you refuse to abide any evil, refuse to live any longer under any circumstances in a world which connives at injustice, can you accept a million from Madam Zachanassian, and thereby fulfil the conditions attaching to her endowment.

(*Thunderous applause.*)

RADIO COMMENTATOR. Just listen to it, ladies and gentlemen, just listen to that applause. We're all overwhelmed. That speech by the Head evinced a moral grandeur we don't find everywhere these days. And a very brave denunciation it was too, aimed at all the little misdemeanours and injustices we find in every community, alas, all over the world.

MAYOR. Alfred Ill ...

RADIO COMMENTATOR. It's the Mayor, I think he's going to take the floor again.

MAYOR. Alfred Ill, I would like to ask you one question.

(*Policeman gives Ill a shove. Ill stands. Radio Commentator crosses with microphone to Ill.*)

RADIO COMMENTATOR. Ah. Now we're going to hear the voice of the man responsible for the Zachanassian endowment: it's the voice of Alfred Ill, our prodigal lady's childhood friend. Alfred Ill — a vigorous man around seventy, an upright Guellener of the old school, and of course he's deeply moved, full of gratitude, full of quiet satisfaction.

MAYOR. Alfred Ill: it is owing to you we have been offered this endowment. Are you aware of that?

(Ill says something in an undertone.)

RADIO COMMENTATOR. My dear sir, would you kindly speak a shade louder, our listeners are so eager to hear you.

ILL. All right.

MAYOR. Will you respect our decision as to acceptance or refusal of the Claire Zachanassian Endowment?

ILL. I shall respect it.

MAYOR. Are there any questions to Alfred Ill?

(Silence.)

The Church?

(Priest says nothing.)

The Medical Profession?

(Doctor says nothing.)

The Police?

(Policeman says nothing.)

The Opposition Party?

(No one says anything.)

I shall now put the issue to vote.

(Silence. Hum of movie-cameras, flash of flash-lights.)

All those pure in heart who want justice done, raise their hands.

(All except Ill raise their hands.)

RADIO COMMENTATOR. There's a devout silence in the auditorium. Nothing but a single sea of hands, all raised, as if making one, mighty pledge for a better, juster world. Only the old man has remained seated, absolutely motionless, he's overcome with joy. His ambition has been fulfilled, and thanks to the generosity of his childhood friend the endowment's finally assured.

MAYOR. The Claire Zachanassian Endowment is accepted. Unanimously. Not for the sake of the money,

CITIZENS. Not for the sake of the money,

MAYOR. But for justice

CITIZENS. But for justice

MAYOR. And for conscience' sake.

CITIZENS. And for conscience' sake.

MAYOR. For we cannot connive at a crime:

CITIZENS. For we cannot connive at a crime:

MAYOR. Let us then root out the wrongdoer,

CITIZENS. Let us then root out the wrongdoer,

MAYOR. And deliver our souls from evil

CITIZENS. And deliver our souls from evil

MAYOR. And all our most sacred possessions.

CITIZENS. And all our most sacred possessions.

ILL (*screams*). My God!

    (*Everyone remains standing solemnly with raised hands, but at this point, however, the news-reel camera jams.*)

CAMERAMAN. What a shame, Mister Mayor. There's a short in the light-cable. Would you just do that last vote again, please?

MAYOR. Do it again?

CAMERAMAN. For the news-reel.

MAYOR. O yes, certainly.

CAMERAMAN. O.K., spots?

A VOICE. O.K.

CAMERAMAN. O.K., shoot!

    (*Mayor assumes pose.*)

MAYOR. The Claire Zachanassian Endowment is accepted. Unanimously. Not for the sake of the money,

CITIZENS. Not for the sake of the money,

MAYOR. But for justice

CITIZENS. But for justice

MAYOR. And for conscience' sake.

CITIZENS. And for conscience' sake.

MAYOR. For we cannot connive at a crime:

CITIZENS. For we cannot connive at a crime:

MAYOR. Let us then root out the wrongdoer,
CITIZENS. Let us then root out the wrongdoer,
MAYOR. And deliver our souls from evil
CITIZENS. And deliver our souls from evil
MAYOR. And all our most sacred possessions.
CITIZENS. And all our most sacred possessions.
  (*Silence.*)
CAMERAMAN (*stage whisper*). Hey! Ill! Come on!
  (*Silence.*)
  (*disappointed*) O.K., so he won't. Pity we didn't get his
  crya joy the first time. That 'My God' was most impressive.

MAYOR. And now we invite the gentlemen of the Press,
  Cinema and Radio to a little Refreshment. In the Res-
  taurant. The easiest way out of the auditorium is through
  the stage-door. Tea is being served for the ladies on the
  Golden Apostle lawn.
    (*Those of the Press, Cinema and Radio cross to background,
    right, and go off. Men of Guellen remain on stage, immobile.
    Ill stands, moves to go.*)
POLICEMAN. You stay here!
    (*He pushes Ill down on to bench.*)
ILL. Were you going to do it today?
POLICEMAN. Of course.
ILL. I'd have thought it would be better at my place.
POLICEMAN. It'll be done here.
MAYOR. No one left in the stalls?
    (*Man Three and Man Four peer down into stalls.*)
MAN THREE. No one.
MAYOR. What about the gallery?
MAN FOUR. Empty.
MAYOR. Lock the doors. Don't let anyone else into the
  auditorium.
    (*Man Three and Man Four step down into stalls.*)

MAN THREE. Locked.

MAN FOUR. Locked.

MAYOR. Put out the lights. ~~The moon is shining through the gallery window. It's enough~~.

(*The stage dims. In the pale moonlight, people are only dimly visible.*)

Form a lane.

(*Men of Guellen form a lane: it ends at Gymnast, clad now in elegant white slacks and vest, round which a red scarf.*)

Father. If you please.

(*Priest crosses slowly to Ill, sits beside him.*)

PRIEST. Now, Ill, your hardest hour is at hand.

ILL. Give me a cigarette.

PRIEST. Mister Mayor, a cigarette.

~~MAYOR (*warmly*). But of course. A good one.~~ [*MO*faid it's a no smoking building

(*Passes packet to Priest, who offers it to Ill, who takes a cigarette; Policeman proffers light, Priest returns packet to Mayor.*)

PRIEST. As the prophet Amos said —

ILL. Please don't.

(*Ill smokes.*)

PRIEST. Are you not afraid?

ILL. Not much, any more.

(*Ill smokes.*)

PRIEST (*helpless*). I'll pray for you.

ILL. Pray for Guellen.

(*Ill smokes. Priest gets slowly to his feet.*)

PRIEST. God have mercy upon us.

(*Priest slowly rejoins the Guelleners' ranks.*)

MAYOR. Alfred Ill. Stand up.

(*Ill hesitates.*)

POLICEMAN. Get up, you bastard.

(*Drags Ill to his feet.*)

MAYOR. Inspector, control yourself.

POLICEMAN. Sorry. It just slipped out.

MAYOR. Alfred Ill. Come here.

> (*Ill drops cigarette, treads it out. Then walks slowly to centre of stage, turns his back to audience.*)

Walk down that lane.

> (*Ill hesitates.*)

POLICEMAN. Get moving.

> (*Ill walks slowly into lane of silent men. When he gets to the end, he comes up against Gymnast planted facing him. Ill stops, turns round, and seeing lane close mercilessly in on him, sinks to his knees. The lane becomes a silent knot of men, swelling up, then slowly crouching down. Silence. Enter Reporters, downstage, left. Lights up.*)

FIRST REPORTER. What's going on here?

> (*The knot of men opens, loosed. The men assemble quietly in background. Only Doctor remains, kneeling beside a corpse over which is spread, as if in an hotel, a chequered table-cloth. Doctor stands, puts away stethoscope.*)

DOCTOR. Heart attack.

> (*Silence.*)

MAYOR. Died of joy.

FIRST REPORTER. Died of joy.

SECOND REPORTER. Life writes the most beautiful stories.

FIRST REPORTER. Better get to work.

> (*Reporters hurry off to background, right. Enter, left, Claire Zachanassian, followed by Butler. She sees corpse, stops, then walks slowly to centre of stage, turns to face audience.*)

CLAIRE ZACHANASSIAN. Bring him here.

> (*Enter Roby and Toby with stretcher, on which they lay Ill, then bring him to Claire Zachanassian's feet.*)
> (*unmoving*) Uncover him, Boby.
> (*Butler uncovers Ill's face. She examines it at length, does not move.*)

Now he looks the way he was, a long while ago: the black panther. Cover him.

(*Butler covers face.*)

Carry him to the coffin.

(*Roby and Toby carry out body, left.*)

Take me to my room, Boby. Get the bags packed. We are going to Capri.

(*Butler offers her his arm, she walks slowly out to left, then stops.*)

Mayor.

(*Mayor emerges from ranks of silent men in background, comes slowly forward.*)

The cheque.

(*She passes him a piece of paper; and exit, with Butler.*)

(*As the clothing, that outward visible form of a mounting standard of living, improves by degrees discreet and unobtrusive yet less and less to be ignored, and as the stage grows more inviting, while rung by rung it scales the social ladder and metamorphoses into wealth, like a gradual change of house from a slum to a well-to-do neighbourhood, so the epitome of that ascent occurs in the concluding tableau. The erstwhile grey and dreary world has been transformed; it has grown rich and dazzling new, a flashy incarnation of up-to-the-minute technics, as if the world and all were ending happily. Flags and streamers, posters, neon-lights now surround the renovated railway station, and the men and women of Guellen clad in evening gowns and dress-suits form two choruses, resembling those of Greek tragedy, nor is this an accident but rather to orientate the close, as if some stricken ship, borne far, far away, were sending out its last signals.*)

CHORUS ONE.

Many, many the monstrous things on earth,
The volcano spewing and spitting its fire,
The shattering earthquake and the tidal wave,
And wars:
      Across the corn the clatter of tanks
      While the radiant mushroom grows
      From the spoor of the atom bomb.

CHORUS TWO.

These monstrous things
      do not exceed
The monstrous plight
      of poverty
Which excites
      no tragic deed
Is not heroic
      but condemns
Our human race
      to barren days
After hopeless
      yesterdays.

THE WOMEN.

The mothers are helpless, they watch
      Their loved ones pining away;

THE MEN.

But the men rumour rebellion.
      The men think treachery.

MAN ONE.

In worn-out shoes they pace the town.

MAN THREE.

A filthy fag-end in their mouths.

CHORUS ONE.

For the jobs, the jobs that earned them bread,
      The jobs are gone.

CHORUS TWO.
And the station scorned by the screaming trains.

ALL.
Now God be praised

MRS ILL.
For kindly fate

ALL.
Has changed all that.

THE WOMEN.
Our tender forms are clad in fitting frocks,

SON.
Young guys with any future drive a Sports,

THE MEN.
The business-men relax in limousines,

DAUGHTER.
All tennis-girls play tennis on hard courts.

DOCTOR.
Our operating-theatres are the best:
The instruments are new, the tiles green;
Medical morale will stand the test.

ALL.
Our suppers now are simmering at home
And Everyman, contented and well-shod,
Buys cigarettes of quality at last.

SCHOOLMASTER.
Assiduous students study their studies,

MAN TWO.
Dynamic tycoons amass fortunes,

ALL.
Rembrandts after Rubens,

PAINTER.
And the painters of today
Get an excellent living in Art.

ACT THREE

PRIEST.

At Christmas and at Easter and at Whitsun
The Cathedral is packed to the portals
With Flocks of the Christian religion.

ALL.

And the trains, the trains come haughtily roaring
     In on the iron
            Railway to Guellen
Hurrying people from town to town,
     Commuting,
          Stopping.

(*Enter Guard, left.*)

GUARD.

Guellen!

STATION-MASTER.

Guellen-Rome Express! All seats please!
     Diner up front!

(*Enter from background Claire Zachanassian seated immobile in sedan-chair, like an old stone idol, and moves down-stage with retinue, between the two Choruses.*)

MAYOR.

Our lady and her noble retinue,

ALL.

Her wealth endowed on Guellen town,

DAUGHTER.

The benefactrice of us all

MAYOR.

Is leaving now!

(*Exit Claire Zachanassian, right, followed last and very slowly by servants bearing coffin.*)

MAYOR.

Long may she live.

ALL.

     She bears a precious charge.

STATION-MASTER.

(Whistles, waves green flag.)

Stand clear!

PRIEST.

Now let us pray to God

ALL.

To protect us all

MAYOR.

In these hustling, booming, prosperous times:

ALL.

Protect all our sacred possessions,
Protect our peace and our freedom,
Ward off the night, nevermore
Let it darken our glorious town
Grown out of the ashes anew.
Let us go and enjoy our good fortune.

POSTSCRIPT

POSTSCRIPT

The Visit is the story of an action which takes place in a small town somewhere in Central Europe. It is told by someone who feels himself at no great remove from the people involved, and who is not so sure he would have acted differently. Any further meaning imputed to the story needs no mention here, and should not be imposed on the stage production. This applies even to the final scene, where the people, admittedly, speak in a more formal fashion than might be found in reality, more in the so-called poetical manner and use what could be described as fine words, but this is merely because the Guelleners have just acquired riches and speak as befits the newly rich, in a more select language. I have described people, not marionettes, an action and not an allegory. I have presented a world, not pointed a moral (as I have been accused of doing), and what is more I have not even tried to force my play on the public, for all that happens quite naturally in any case, so long as the audience too belong in the theatre. In my view, a play is acted in the theatre according to the limits and possibilities of the stage; it is not confined within the garb of some special style. When the Guelleners act trees, therefore, this is no Surrealism. Rather is it a somewhat distressing love-story, enacted in that wood: an old man's attempt to approach an old woman; and this is placed in a 'poetical' setting in order to make it more bearable. I write with an inherent confidence in the theatre and its actors — this is my fundamental inspiration; the material draws me into its charmed circle. To play his character, the actor needs little: only the very outer skin, the text, which of course accords with it. That is to say, just as any creature is sealed off inside its skin, so the play is sealed off inside speech. For speech is all the dramatist provides. It is his end-product. And it is consequently impossible to work on

the element of speech alone, but only on that which gives rise
to speech, namely thought and action; only dilettantes work
on speech alone. I think the actor should aim to present that
end-product afresh, whereby all that is art should seem to be
nature. If the foreground I have provided be correctly
played, the background will emerge of its own accord. I
don't account myself a member of the contemporary avant-
garde. I admit I have my Theory of Art as well, it's a thing
one doesn't always enjoy having, and inasmuch as it's my
own private opinion I withhold it (otherwise I'd be obliged
to practise it) and prefer being regarded as a somewhat lunatic
child of nature lacking a proper sense of form and structure.
Producers and directors will probably come nearest the mark
if they stage my plays after the style of folk-plays, and treat
me as a kind of conscious Nestroy. They should follow the
flights of my fancy and let the deeper meanings take care of
themselves; they should change the sets without pause or
curtain, play even the car scene simply and for preference with
a stage-vehicle, equipped only with what the action requires:
seats, steering-wheel, bumpers, the car seen from the front,
rear seats raised and, of course, everything brand-new, like
the shoes, etc. (This scene hasn't anything to do with Wilder
— why not? Dialectical exercise for critics.) Claire Zachanassian doesn't represent Justice or the Marshall Plan or even the
Apocalypse, she's purely and simply what she is, namely, the
richest woman in the world and, thanks to her finances, in a
position to act as the Greek tragic heroines acted, absolutely,
terribly, something like Medea. She can afford to. This lady
has a sense of humour and it mustn't be overlooked, for she is
quite as detached from people as from saleable objects and
detached from herself as well, and she has a rare grace, more,
she has a wicked charm. None the less, moving as she does
outside the human pale, she has grown into someone unalter-
able and rigid, contains within herself no further possibility

of development and she, in consequence, is cast in a mould of stone, she is the one to be represented as a stone idol. She's a poetical apparition, so is her retinue, and her eunuchs too. The latter are not to be given a realistically unappetizing interpretation, complete with high-pitched gelded voices, but made on the contrary to seem quite improbable, legendary, fantastic, soft and ghostly in their vegetable contentment, a sacrifice to total revenge, logical as the law-books of antiquity. (To facilitate the playing of these roles the blind pair may speak alternately, instead of together, in which case they needn't repeat every phrase.) While Claire Zachanassian, fixed and unmoving, is a heroine from the very beginning, her onetime sweetheart still has to develop into a hero. At first, a disreputable shopkeeper, he is her unsuspecting victim and, guilty, believes life has been its own expiation of that guilt; he is a thoughtless figure of a man, a simple man in whose mind something slowly dawns, by the agency of fear and terror, something highly personal; a man who in recognizing his guilt lives out justice and who, in death, achieves greatness. (His death should not be without a certain monumental quality.) That death is both meaningful and meaningless. It would only have been entirely meaningful in the mythological kingdom of some ancient *polis*. But the action of this story unfolds in Guellen. In the present. The Guelleners who swarm round the hero are people like the rest of us. They must not, emphatically not, be portrayed as wicked. At first, they are firmly resolved to reject the offer, and although they incur debts that is not because they intend to kill Ill, but out of thoughtless irresponsibility and the feeling that somehow things will come to a happy settlement. Act Two should be directed accordingly. And then in the station scene, Ill is the only one to see his own plight and be afraid; not a harsh word has yet been uttered; events only take their decisive turn during the scene in Petersens' Barn. Disaster can no longer be averted. From that moment onward, the Guelleners steadily pave their way to the murder, waxing indignant over Ill's guilt, etc. The family alone keep on to the end trying to convince themselves things will somehow turn out all right; for they aren't wicked either, only weak, like everyone. It's a community slowly yielding to temptation, as in the Schoolmaster's case; but it must be a perceptible yielding. The temptation is too strong, the poverty too wretched. The old lady is a wicked creature, and for precisely that reason mustn't be played wicked, she has to be rendered as human as possible, not with anger but with sorrow and humour, for nothing could harm this comedy with a tragic end more than heavy seriousness.

F. D.

ADDENDA

The second shop-scene (Act Three, pp. 67 ff.) may be simpli-
fied by omission of Painter. So staged, a further alteration
(p. 73) is required: 'SCHOOLMASTER. Child, you disappoint me.
It was up to you to speak out, and now your old schoolmaster
must unleash the voice of thunder! I protest! I wish to make
a public appeal to world opinion! Guellen is planning a
monstrous deed!' Remaining excisions will quickly be
located. Similarly (p. 73) the following insertion: after
'MAN ONE. Have you gone mad? MAN TWO. Stop him!', read:
'FIRST REPORTER. Hey, folks, let the gennelman have his say.'
It is also possible to cast only one Reporter.